KU-204-055

DURHAM CATHEDRAL

TRAVEL TO LANDMARKS

DURHAM CATHEDRAL

Debra Shipley
Photographs by Angelo Hornak

Tauris Parke Books, London

The author would like to thank the following for their help in the production of this book: at Durham, the Dean and Chapter, Canon Ronald L. Coppin, Canon Tony Hart, Mr Denis Trigg, Mr Ian Curry, Mr Roger Norris, Miss Wendy Stevenson, Mr Denis Welsh, Mr Owen Rees; from UNESCO Ms Anne Sieve; Martin Bolton; and the Surtees Society for permission to quote from *Rites of Durham*. Finally, I want to say thank you to Simon Molesworth for his constant support and encouragement.

Published by Tauris Parke Books
110 Gloucester Avenue, London NW1 8JA
In association with KEA Publishing Services Ltd., London

TRAVEL TO LANDMARKS

Series Editor: Judy Spours
Editorial Assistant: Elizabeth Harcourt
Designer: David Robinson
Maps by John Hewitt
All photographs by Angelo Hornak except pages 9, 10, 17, 118.

British Library Cataloguing in Publication Data
Shipley, Debra
Durham Cathedral. – (Travel to Landmarks).
1. Durham, (County). Durham. Cathedrals: Durham Cathedral, history.
I. Title II. Series 942.865

ISBN 1–85043–220–1

Photosetting by: Litho Link Ltd., Welshpool, Powys, UK.
Colour Separations by: Fabbri, Milan, Italy.
Printed by: Fabbri, Milan, Italy.

FRONTISPIECE This stonework is quintessentially Durham, showing the alternation of decorated cylindrical piers and the cluster forms of the composite pier. The simple detailing of the capital is similar on both forms, providing the base for the springing of the quadripartite vaulting system. This view looks west along the north nave aisle.

Contents

Introduction

Viewed from the south-west, the cathedral's western towers and the top portion of the Galilee Chapel rise above the River Wear. The scale of their high defensive position is dramatized by the Old Fulling Mill below, which is now a museum of archaeology.

OVERLEAF Durham's commanding position is clearly demonstrated in this aerial view. Its impressive bulk dominates the high spur of land protected by the River Wear, which loops around it. The cathedral's huge size is emphasized by the more domestically scaled monastic buildings to its south and the relatively small Norman keep to its north.

Durham Cathedral is Europe's most important Romanesque church, a UNESCO World Heritage Site, and the jewel of northern England. Its architecture ranks high in world terms, and the innovative nature of its construction attracts attention from numerous experts across the globe. This, coupled with its geographically dramatic site, high on a rocky plateau protected by a loop in the River Wear and by a castle which for centuries was the focus of government administration in the north, makes the cathedral a major monument to England's rich cultural history. The process of stripping back the years and conjuring up an image in the mind's eye of Durham before human habitation reveals a changing landscape and a layering of history which has served to enrich the region's, and eventually the cathedral's, architectural heritage.

Earliest human occupation of the area seems to have taken place during late Mesolithic times (*c.* 5300–3200 BC), but only a few flints from the period have so far been found. Then, around 3000 BC, these hunter-gatherer people began to clear the land to provide grazing for their animals. During the Neolithic period (*c.* 3200–2000), a definite shift towards a more settled way of life seems to have taken place, and there is evidence of cereal cultivation throughout the county. The burial remains of Neolithic folk – a round barrow at East Murton, a long barrow at Ireshopeburn, a causeway camp at Hastings Hill – indicate the likelihood that the communities were ritualistic in at least part of their social structure. Remains of Beaker burials (*c.* 2500–1500 BC) have been uncovered at Sherburn Grange, Kelloe Law and West Brandon, which suggests that the Beaker and the late Neolithic peoples inhabited the area for overlapping periods. Furthermore, as the Neolithic time gave way to the Bronze Age (*c.* 1750–700 BC), the Beakers once again co-existed with different people; how well this worked for those involved cannot be evaluated. The majority of the Bronze Age finds are burial sites – East Murton, Copt Hill, Crawley Edge – and there are a number of standing stones which imply ritualistic practices. Bronze Age style stock farming continued into the Iron Age (*c.* 700 BC – AD 70), but there is a marked absence of burial archaeology, suggesting that inhumation practices changed in favour of cremation. Defended settlements do, however, make an appearance at Maiden Castle, Shackleton, Becon and Redworth amongst others.

Roman occupation brought about major changes in both agriculture

and defensive fort construction and introduced the notion of travelling distances by permanent roadways. The Romans intensively cultivated cereals throughout the whole region of Durham and they constructed forts at Piercebridge, Binchester, Lanchester and Ebchester, while, to connect their strongholds, they engineered a major north-south road known as Dere Street. Joining it, at intervals, were a number of other roads linking with the forts at Greta Bridge, South Shields and Chester-le-Street, creating a formidable communication network and thus strengthening their power structure.

The transitional period between the Roman occupation and the early medieval period is still hazy. Finds have been both few and hard to date. More evidence is, however, available for the seventh century, the time when the rapidly expanding and organizing Christian religion, needing permanent buildings, began to construct churches and monastic complexes. The area around the high plateau on which Durham Cathedral was to be sited was scattered with villages whose surviving seventh and eighth century names give clues as to their character: Shadforth meaning shallow ford: Cassop, valley of the cats; Sherburn, bright burn; and Shincliffe, cliff of ghosts. The area of Durham now known as Elvet was once a village in its own right and, it seems, an important one for it was here on 17 July 763 that Peohtwine was consecrated Bishop of Whithorne.

At that time, life in the region must have been harsh. The environment would certainly have been wild and unforgiving at times, particularly during the cold northern winters, but it was not a totally untamed land. Cultivation of some type or other had existed for thousands of years, a relatively sophisticated road system had improved communications, and the area's great natural resources – wood, various sandstones, limestone and marble – made building a viable proposition.

This, then, was the setting for the construction of one of the greatest cathedrals ever built. It was a place of ancient heritage, of established Christianity and of abundant raw materials. However, additional motivation was needed to produce architecture of such excellence; at Durham it took the form of conflict, status, power and patronage, each interwoven with the pervasive qualities of myth and religion. From the struggles in all their forms, a building emerged that was atmospherically special and also architecturally unique – Durham Cathedral.

1 Legends, Faith and Fortifications

During a tour of the north of England, J.M.W. Turner filled sketch books with atmospheric images such as this dramatically lit interior view of the cathedral, looking east along the south aisle, dated *c.* 1797-8 (detail shown here). It is executed in watercolour, pencil and gouache. Courtesy Tate Gallery, London.

Today Durham Cathedral impresses itself as strongly as ever on both the eye and the imagination, and it is the same image as has been observed, recorded and perpetuated by artists over the last few centuries. Their paintings, which capture the power and beauty of the cathedral, remain representative of many visitors' first and most lasting impressions. Thomas Girtin's watercolour of 1798, depicting a majestic religious edifice reaching up to silver-blue heavens and dominating the more earthly medieval town below, which crumbles into darkness, sums up many people's experience of visiting Durham. Then there's J. S. Cotman's watercolour of 1805, which shows a more earthbound building of huge proportions, framed with greenery and once again blessed with rays of sunlight, whilst all beneath are shrouded with shadows. Or there's J. M. W. Turner's very special vision. In a watercolour dated 1835, Turner took the symbolic light/dark abstraction further; in his painting the cathedral became a blaze of etherial light, its towers and roofs just picked out, whilst everything below it was reduced to a blur of darkness. All these artists, and the numerous visitors to the cathedral, share a common experience; they all respond to the overwhelming physical qualities of the architecture and its dramatic setting.

From whichever direction it was approached, Durham stunned its eighteenth and nineteenth century visitors, as it does its twentieth century ones. Situated high on a rocky plateau, surrounded by swooping verdant slopes, the cathedral site is almost moated by the River Wear, which loops around it forming a close neck on the lea side and a deep gorge at the scarp. Despite the development of Durham city around the citadel, the romantic power of the cathedral's position has not been affected; the present-day visitor can still experience the same vistas recorded by earlier travellers. For one such traveller, Daniel Defoe, Durham was, '. . . surrounded almost with the River Wear, which with the castle standing on an eminence, encloses the city in the middle of it; as the castle does, also the cathedral, the bishop's palace, and the fine houses of the clergy' (1724). Similarly, Matthew Arnold wrote, '. . . when you cross the River Wear by the Prebends bridge and, ascending through its beautiful skirt of wood, plant yourself on the hill opposite the cathedral, the view of the cathedral and castle together is superb; even Oxford has no view to compare with it . . .' (letter 1861) – praise indeed from the poet and essayist. Samuel Johnson's reaction was

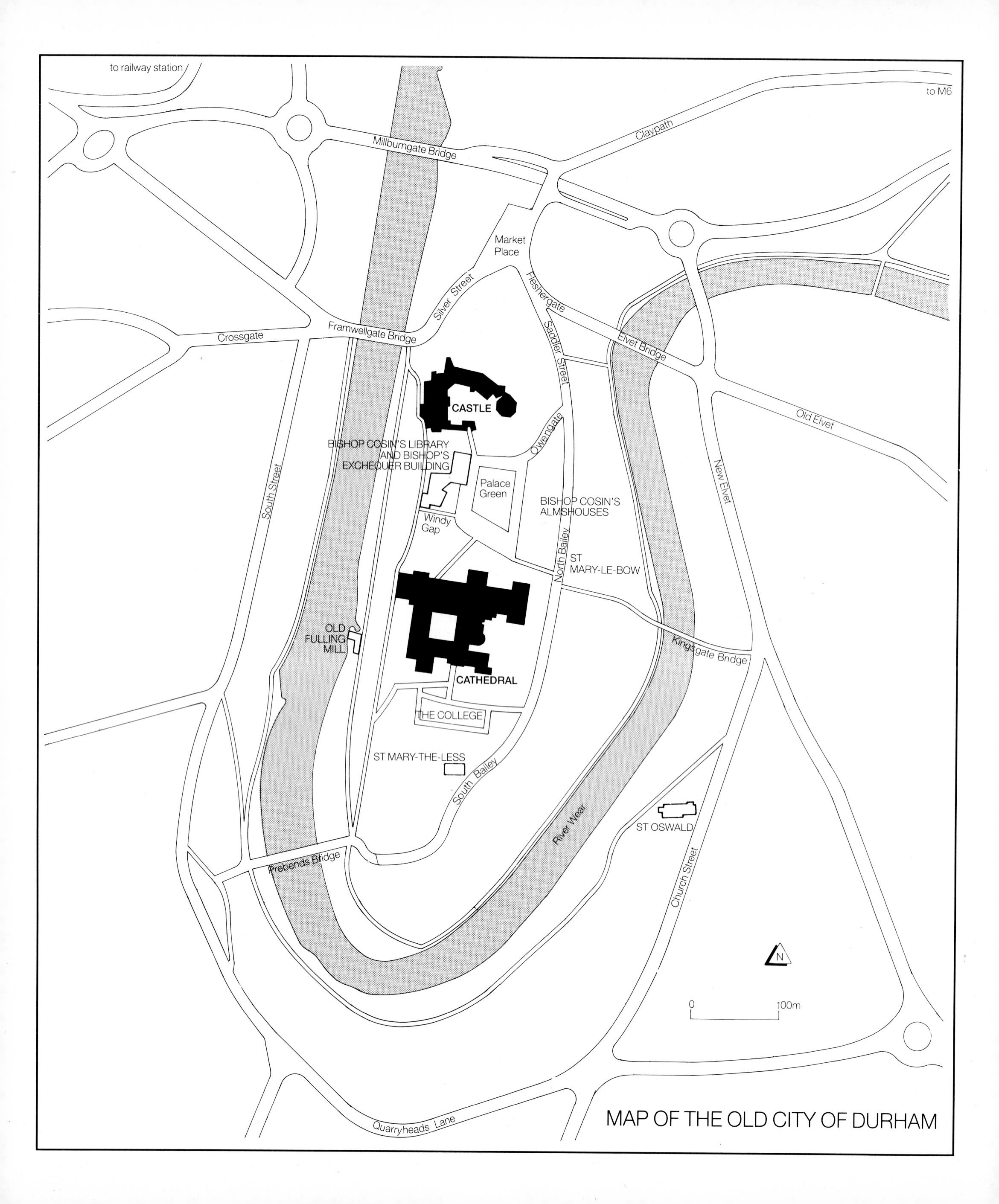
to railway station
to M6
Claypath
Millburngate Bridge
Market
Place
Silver Street
Fleshergate
Crossgate
Framwellgate Bridge
Saddler Street
Elvet Bridge
CASTLE
Old Elvet
Owengate
BISHOP COSIN'S LIBRARY
AND BISHOP'S
EXCHEQUER BUILDING
Palace
Green
New Elvet
South Street
BISHOP COSIN'S
ALMSHOUSES
Windy
Gap
North Bailey
ST
MARY-LE-BOW
OLD
FULLING
MILL
Kingsgate Bridge
CATHEDRAL
THE COLLEGE
ST MARY-THE-LESS
South Bailey
ST OSWALD
River Wear
Prebends Bridge
Church Street
N
0
100m
Quarryheads Lane
MAP OF THE OLD CITY OF DURHAM

less favourable; he considered the cathedral to be 'a gloomy pile'. More recently, Nikolaus Pevsner described the view of Durham, its cathedral and castle, as, 'one of the great experiences of Europe'. These writers were moved by the unique grouping of buildings on a very particular site and, whether in condemnation or praise, the physicality of the place demanded their attention.

The legend of St Cuthbert

The spectacle provided by the cathedral and castle is of Norman origin, designed and built by craftsmen brought over from France. However, the story of its creation starts not with the Normans in Durham, nor even in France, but with a small community of Anglo-Saxon monks on the windswept island of Lindisfarne (Holy Island) which lies just off the north-east coast of Northumberland, not far from Berwick-upon-Tweed.

During the mid-seventh century, Lindisfarne was presided over by Bishop Cuthbert who, legend has it, was once a shepherd boy from the Borders. It is said that while still only a boy, tending his flock on the hills of Lammermoor, Cuthbert saw a vision of the soul of St Aidan being taken to heaven by angels. Believing this to be a sign from God, Cuthbert decided to become a monk and chose the life of a hermit. Later, however, by popular demand, he eventually became a bishop. He was consecrated Bishop of Lindisfarne in 685. Just two years later he died and was buried in the small church on Lindisfarne.

Archaeological exploration has, as yet, discovered few remains of that Anglo-Saxon monastic settlement, and little is known of its architecture. However, using what remains are available and drawing on knowledge of other comparable sites, such as that on Iona, experts have been able to construct a possible picture. The Hiberno-Scottish settlement on Iona was the parent house of the Lindisfarne monastery, so it is thought that it might have provided the model for the Lindisfarne plan. However, its most prominent feature – the *vallum monasterii* (the boundary between the monastery and secular buildings) – appears to be absent on Lindisfarne. This barrier, in the form of a bank, was significant in that it marked both a spiritual and a physical separation. It was often quite extensive, enclosing not only the immediate monastic buildings but also the gardens and fields which belonged to the settlement. Today, a ruined priory church can be seen

Ever since the remains of St Cuthbert were brought to Durham, his shrine has been a place of pilgrimage. As the power and importance of the cathedral that they established increased, so the numbers of visitors to the tomb, bringing gifts, multiplied. All sorts of treasures were accumulated, but more unusual gifts included part of the rod of Moses; a fragment from the holy manger; part of the throne of the twelve apostles; and a claw of a griffin. Today St Cuthbert's shrine is an altogether simpler affair. His tomb lies beneath a grey marble slab behind the Neville Screen.

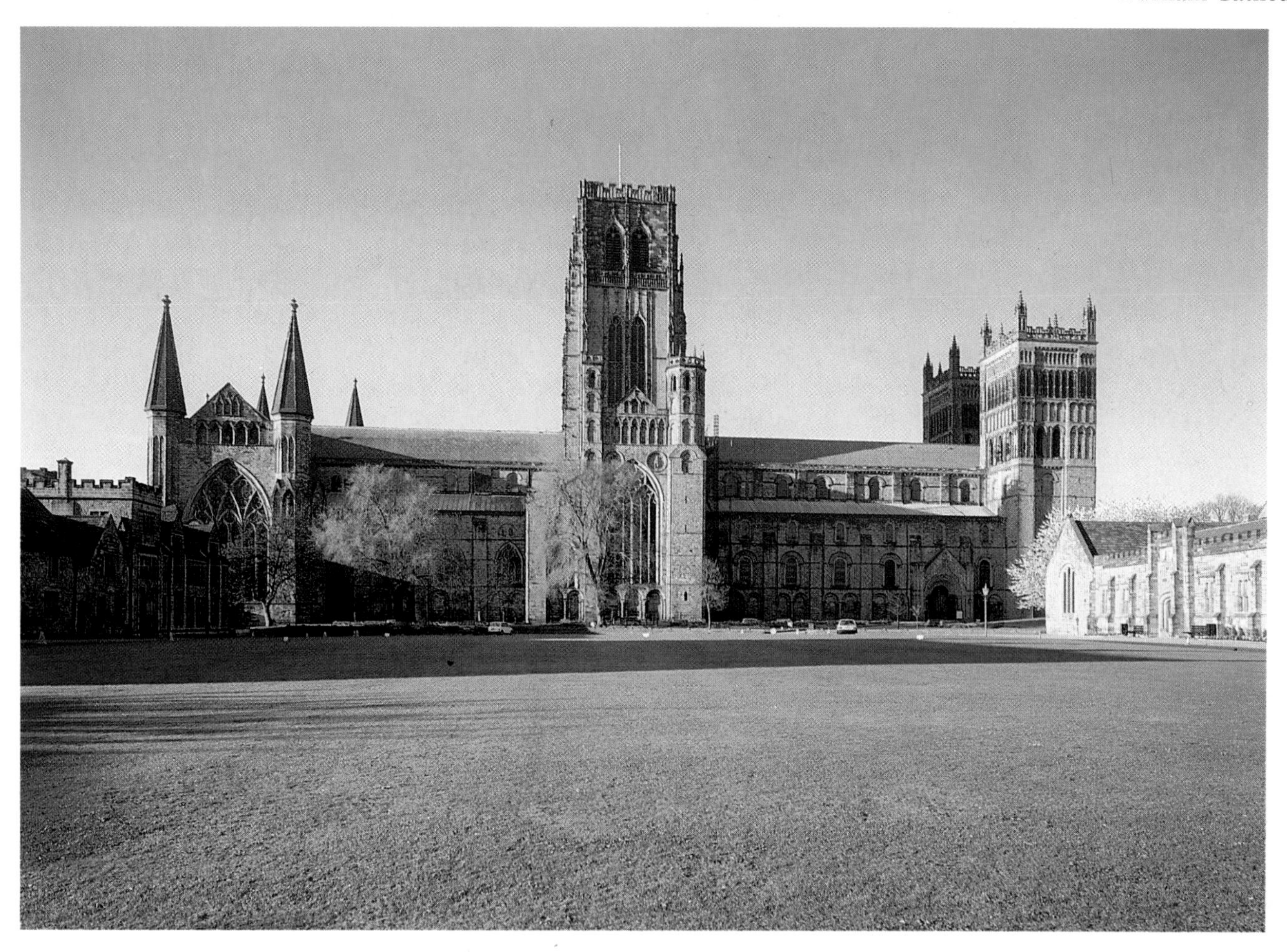

ABOVE Long shadows are cast across Palace Green, which offers an unhindered view of the entire length of the cathedral's north side.

RIGHT On the external north wall of the Transept of the Nine Altars is an eighteenth-century sculpture known as Dun Cow. The most likely interpretation of the rather spiritless motif is that the milkmaids and their cow were a symbol of the cathedral's prosperity.

OVERLEAF J.M.W. Turner painted this evocative image from a popular vantage spot on Prebends Bridge. The picture is not, however, a faithful reproduction of the scene, but is instead a slightly wide angle rendering which distorts the cathedral's scale to add a sense of the sublime. Courtesy National Galleries of Scotland.

which was probably constructed over the site of the principal church of the original monastery. It is known from the writing of the contemporary historian, the Venerable Bede, that the monastic complex included two churches, a watchtower, a dormitory and a guesthouse. Bede also mentions a retreat, used by Cuthbert, sited on the small tidal islet to the south-west of Lindisfarne, known today as St Cuthbert's Island.

During his lifetime Cuthbert was said to be an exceptionally good man and after his death he was called a saint. Some 10 years after his burial, Cuthbert's body was exhumed and it was discovered that it had not decayed in the normal way after death. It was enclosed in a shrine above ground, and became a holy relic revered by the monks on Lindisfarne for around 200 years. In the late ninth century, persistent raids by the Danes forced the monks to flee from their island. Cuthbert, before his death, had told them that if they ever left Lindisfarne they must take his bones with them. Accordingly, in preparation for the exodus, his faithful followers opened Cuthbert's shrine and found to their amazement that his body, after two centuries, was still perfectly preserved. They made a wooden coffin to transport the incorrupt body and left Lindisfarne in search of a new sanctuary and a resting-place for their saintly relic.

The founding of a Christian community at Durham

After much wandering (many of the churches in the north of England are dedicated to St Cuthbert; they are said to have been constructed at places where the monks rested for a while with their precious burden), the monks finally stopped at Chester-le-Street, about 6 miles from Durham. They established a settlement which survived for over a hundred years, but in 995 further raiding caused the religious community to resume their wandering. They went as far as Ripon before returning north once more, coming at last to Durham. According to legend, Cuthbert's coffin became immovable near Durham, so the monks fasted and prayed for guidance. Eventually, so the tale goes, the monks received a holy communication that Cuthbert wished his final resting-place to be 'Dunholm' – hill island.

There could have been more astute political reasons for the choice of Durham. The monks' leader, Bishop Aldhune, had powerful family connections in the area. His daughter was married to Uchted, heir of the

ABOVE AND RIGHT The remains of the Venerable Bede rest in the Galilee Chapel. Bede was a scholar notable for his work, *The Church History of English People*. He died in 735, and in 1022 his by then saintly remains were stolen by a sacrist at Durham. Bede lies in a plain tomb chest which has a black marble top. At the four corners of the marble are large, sixteenth-century candlesticks which have recently been restored.

LEFT The south front, the most domestic face of the cathedral.

SAINT · CVTHBERT
S: CVTHBERT PREACHES IN A MOVNTAIN VILLAGE
S: CVTHBERT PRAYS BEFORE HIS CELL IN THE FARNE ISLAND

This is one of a series of late nineteenth-century windows which were commissioned as part of the restoration work carried out by Sir George Gilbert Scott. It shows something of the life of St Cuthbert, the hermit who became Bishop of Lindisfarne and around whom the story of the foundation of Durham Cathedral is based. In this depiction, Cuthbert is preaching in a mountain village and praying for guidance in front of his cell. Other windows in the series feature the Venerable Bede, Benedict Biscop, who was an important seventh-century patron of the arts, St Aidan, Bishop of Lindisfarne (635-651) and St Paulinus (584-644), who converted King Edwin to Christianity in 627.

Earl of Northumberland, and at Durham the community would be under the protection of Uchted. Whatever their reasoning, the monks soon set about building a new shrine for St Cuthbert. At first it took the form of a simple construction made from the boughs of nearby trees. This temporary structure housed the relic until a sturdier building could be erected, probably also from timber, which became known as the White Church. The White Church sheltered the relic for about 3 years, during which time a great stone church, also called the White Church, was built. Bishop Aldhune dedicated it in 998, and the incorrupt body of St Cuthbert was translated to it. It is reported by the chronicler Simeon, that when Aldhune died in 1017 only the west tower of the great White Church was unfinished. The new shrine quickly became a site of pilgrimage for the poor, the rich, and the famous alike. King Canute was an early visitor, and he granted numerous privileges and great tracts of land to the religious community.

Durham's easily defendable position, dominated by its Saxon cathedral – a symbol of both secular and religious power – quickly attracted a thriving population. The community developed to form a town which clustered around the cathedral and sprawled down the hill away from it. The relative safety of Durham's position provided the religious community with some respite from the constant fear of invasion, but William of Normandy was not to be deterred. In 1066 his forces swept across the south of England suppressing all before them, and Robert Cumin was sent with 700 men to take the northern territory. Cumin and his army entered Durham and made camp for the night, but the local people surrounded the citadel and at dawn attacked and killed the occupying Norman forces, burning Cumin to death.

William himself then came north and wreaked great vengeance on the people of the region in retribution for their stand against him. On William's orders, every dwelling between York and Durham was raised to the ground, and every person caught by the Norman soldiers was killed. In very real fear for their lives, the Bishop and religious community at Durham fled to Lindisfarne, taking the body of St Cuthbert with them. However, when they reached the crossing place, they found the tide was high and Lindisfarne was cut off and could be reached only by boat, which the monks did not possess. So they waited and prayed to St Cuthbert, and in the morning it seemed their prayers had been answered for the tide had receded to allow them safe passage;

it was, to them, a miracle worked by their saint. In reality, the community had been away from their original home for so long they had forgotten that Lindisfarne's access route was tidal, and that crossings were therefore only possible at low tide.

It seems that the monks did not stay on Lindisfarne for long, but instead returned to Durham. When William arrived, after battling with Scotland, and demanded to see their famous relic, the monks were able to say that the incorrupt body was in its shrine. William gave orders for the shrine to be opened so that he might see for himself the miraculous remains. This was a serious sacreligious act, and it was apparent to everyone that when William became ill with fever on the day the shrine was due to be opened, St Cuthbert was responsible, angry that his remains were to be violated. It is said that William, frightened, took flight for York, and St Cuthbert's shrine remained unopened.

Norman occupation brought great changes to the religious establishment at Durham. Bishop Aethelwin was discredited, left his see and met an ignominious end. He fled first to Scotland, possibly taking some of the community's treasures with him to pay his way. Then, after wintering in Scotland, he made his way south once more, but was caught at Ely and taken to Abingdon where he was imprisoned on the King's orders and eventually starved to death. In Durham, a strict Benedictine Order of monks replaced the existing community and new building work was begun, changes that were introduced by the first Norman bishop, Bishop Walcher of Lorraine, and continued by his successor, William of St Carileph.

Bishop Carileph had been abbot of St Vincent, and before that a monk at the Benedictine abbey of St Carileph, from whence he took his name. Carileph had a great ambition: he wanted to replace the simple Saxon cathedral with a splendid new one more worthy of his extensive, newly acquired see.

It would seem that Bishop Carileph was an accomplished negotiator and schemer. He was a minister of William Rufus and was well regarded by him. However, Carileph became involved in the suspicions and intrigues of court, where he spent a good deal of his time. When he became associated with the rebellion of Odo of Bayeux, he was forced to flee to Normandy for refuge, and remained there for several years until he managed to do the king a service and regain his former position of favour. It seems that while he was in Normandy he developed his

A haze of blossom heralds spring and contrasts with the heavy form of the west towers, which are each 144 feet high.

Sculpture of 'The Upper Room,' in which twelve tree trunks – elms killed by Dutch Elm Disease – represent the Twelve Apostles. The sculptor, Colin Milbourn, has provided a three-dimensional puzzle which can only be solved by sitting in a chair carved from a thirteenth tree. From this viewpoint the images combine to give a perspective of the room where the Last Supper took place. There are many details – notice Judas's purse containing the pieces of silver in the nearest window on the left.

idea for a sumptuous cathedral, for when he eventually returned to England, be brought with him sacred objects for his new church. Ostensibly, Carileph intended to build a great cathedral which would honour the remains of St Cuthbert whilst simultaneously creating an edifice which would promote his own personal status and symbolize his power.

In 1092 the shrine of St Cuthbert was dismantled to make room for the new cathedral. The holy relic was held in a temporary shrine until a permanent place was constructed for it behind the high altar of the new building (not that all went well with the move; a chronicler recorded that the night before the relic was to be moved, the sturdy timbering which supported the vault over the new shrine fell to the floor, and it was claimed that St Cuthbert was responsible). In the same year building work began on the cathedral. Masons and craftsmen were brought over from Normandy to accomplish the skilled work involved, living in special sheds and 'loges', while the real graft of clearing the site, quarrying the stone, felling trees for timber, making lime, and laying the foundations was performed by the forced labour of the indigenous Saxon community.

Durham's natural defences

Fortification plays an important part in Durham's story. Archaeological excavations suggest that Durham was a chosen vantage point long before the protectors of St Cuthbert's body settled on it. As mentioned earlier, numerous communities had occupied the vicinity at different times, including the fort-building Iron Age people who constructed complicated defensive systems. Maiden Castle, a typically Iron Age promontory fort, is one such fortification. It vies with the Durham Peninsula as a likely site for Caer Weir, the legendary fortress of the Saxon invaders mentioned in Welsh bardic accounts. Firmer evidence for the early settlement of Durham came in 1974 with the excavations of the steep slope (now Saddler Street) leading up to the summit. The dig revealed the remains of circular wattle dwellings dating from the tenth century.

When the first timber church was built, the natural defences of the site were strengthened by deep ditches, banks and, probably, wooden ramparts. Around 1072, the occupying Normans encircled the whole tongue of land with stone defences and built a great castle. It was

LEFT Construction of the Galilee Chapel meant that the great west door, formerly the main entrance to the cathedral, became largely obsolete. In the fifteenth century it was closed up and the space created by its recessed opening was used as a site for Bishop Langley's altar and monument. Langley had chosen a prominent setting for his monument and its design, and the construction was to be no less so. The large tomb chest is centrally placed, flanked by steps to the right and left which lead up to the altar. Now simple and open, until 1846 it had a wooden reredos, and two nave bays were once enclosed by stone screens to form a small chapel.

RIGHT On the oak door of the present main public entrance to the cathedral is a replica of the twelfth-century sanctuary ring (the original is on display in the treasury). It has a great tradition, for during the Middle Ages a criminal could ask for asylum by knocking on the door with the huge sanctuary ring. In a small room above the door, two men were available at night to admit individuals and toll the bell to tell the people of Durham that someone was seeking sanctuary. The criminal would then be given a black gown to wear and be provided with food and somewhere to sleep in a railed-off alcove beneath the south-west tower. He could decide either to stand trial or to leave the country within forty days.

Durham Castle keep sits on top of a small motte overlooking Palace Green below. The castle is approached via a Norman gateway (not shown) and a former dry moat. It retains a Norman undercroft chapel, but the exterior was faced in the eighteenth century by James Wyatt.

positioned at the neck of the loop in the river, the only part of the site not protected by a steep escarpment.

William recognized the strategic advantages of the region and chose it as his major administrative centre in the north of England. To oversee his dangerous new borderlands, which had a rebellious reputation and which were regularly attacked by the Scots, William instituted a palatinate. It was ruled by a Norman prince-bishop who possessed full royal powers, including the right to have his own army, judiciary, mint, exchequer and parliament.

Thus, through legend, faith and fortification, Durham became a mighty symbol of both the church and the military. Tales of the incorrupt remains of St Cuthbert are interwoven with the very real powers of the day – the church and the monarch. At Durham the two positions of military ruler and religious leader were combined in that of palatine. The plateau site was developed to make full use of its dramatic and dominating setting. The encircling battlements and natural defences of rock and water combined to protect, both symbolically and actually, an area in which military and religious buildings co-existed. The Normans stamped their presence on Durham with a castle, bridges over the fording points of the River Wear (Framwellgate Bridge, and Elvet Bridge) and, most significantly, a cathedral. This cathedral was an important and ambitious undertaking because, with its construction, the Normans not only created an imposing symbol of their power, they also succeeded in inventing a whole new form of building.

2 Cathedral Construction

Carved patterns on cylindrical columns: vertical flutes in the south nave aisle (*TOP LEFT*); chevron-shaped design in the nave (*TOP RIGHT*); spiral patterning on the north transept column (*CENTRE LEFT AND RIGHT*); diaper patterning in the south nave aisle (*BOTTOM LEFT*); and a chevron-shaped design in the south nave aisle (*BOTTOM RIGHT*). The designs were made in separate sections, and then assembled around the columns.

The significance of Durham Cathedral lies both in the quantity of the surviving Norman structure and in the quality and innovative nature of the building work. The majority of the building which survives today is the work of Norman craftsmen brought over to England by Bishop Carileph. In 1093 work began under his direction (it is thought that the unknown architect responsible for the designs may even have been Carileph himself), but in 1096 he died and his plans for a magnificent cathedral were taken over by his successor, Ralph Flambard. Flambard was William Rufus's chaplain and his most powerful minister, and under his zealous stewardship work progressed quickly, the cathedral emerging, more or less complete, in just 40 years. It was a triumph of building management.

As with most large and important churches, work on Durham began at the eastern end with the construction of the choir – the most vital area for the observance of religious offices. It was completed in the early twelfth century and its high vaulted space must have seemed courageous to contemporary viewers. Unfortunately, fissures developed in the vaulting, and it was replaced in the thirteenth century. The vaulting of the choir aisles, however, has survived to testify to the success of the enormous technical innovations attempted at Durham from the outset of its construction.

By 1104 the vault of the high altar was completed and money had run out. The remains of St Cuthbert could, however, be placed in their newly erected shrine which was positioned just a few feet behind the high altar. Before its repositioning, the saint's coffin was opened in order that his remains might be examined, initially by Prior Turgot and nine of his monks, and then by the Abbot of Seez. After a solemn *Te Deum*, procession, and numerous speeches by Flambard, the body was found to be incorrupt. Once installed in the cathedral, in a sumptuous shrine which could be visited by the public, St Cuthbert again became the focus for pilgrims, who provided a bountiful source of revenue.

By 1110 money had been found to stone vault the northern transept but the south transept was simply encased by a timber roof. Over the next 15 years Bishop Flambard ensured that funds were forthcoming to construct the nave and to stone vault the south transept. By 1135 the nave and its aisles were complete.

LEFT The view from the tower gallery shows the marble floor of the choir designed by Scott between 1870 and 1875.

The choir aisles were completed in 1104 as part of the first phase of Norman building. Originally these north (*ABOVE LEFT*) and south (*ABOVE RIGHT*) aisles each terminated with a small apse flanking the larger central apse of the choir. Their cross-rib vaulting is the earliest surviving in the cathedral.

ABOVE The choir aisles have blank arcading formed from a series of intersecting arches which spring from slim coupled shafts. Such Norman wall embellishment was, at the beginning of the twelfth century, at a very early stage of development, which makes its assured handling and the relatively large-scale proportions of what is effectively a dado decoration impressive.

RIGHT This view east along the south choir aisle to the Transept of Nine Altars shows the division of the bays by transverse arches. The eleventh-century arches are rounded in form, except for those of the last bay which, built during the construction of the Transept of Nine Altars in the thirteenth century, are of pointed design. The tomb on the north side is the back elevation of Bishop Hatfield's chantry and his Bishop's Throne. The latter is said to be the highest of its kind.

LEFT The quadripartite vaulting in the choir dates from the thirteenth century. It replaces a similar structure which was the first of its type to be built.

RIGHT Massive Norman piers, designed to carry the weight of the central tower, rise on either side of the north transept at the crossing, which rests on four great arches. The arches to the right open onto the south aisle, which is subdivided into chapels including one dedicated to the Durham Light Infantry.

LEFT Note the ribs high up in the south transept which, unlike those of the north transept, are decorated with a zigzag design which is thought to be the first instance of its use in England.

RIGHT The thistle which surmounts this gilded clock may have saved it from destruction. In the mid-seventeenth century Scottish prisoners were held in the cathedral with little food and no heating. They burnt everything wooden except this clock. They may have revered the Scottish thistle emblem. The clock was erected by Prior Castell during his time at Durham, 1494-1519.

Early Norman building innovations

The Norman masons found inspiration for their building methods in the churches of Lombardy. From antiquity onwards the Lombards had had a reputation as skilful builders. During the eleventh century they travelled Europe selling their expertise and moving their workshops from site to site. Seeking an alternative to the basilicas of the early Christian tradition, the Lombards introduced square bays and strong piers into their church construction. Because of the fire risk inherent in wooden roofs, stone was starting to be used and the piers had to be massive to support the great weight of a stone roof. Contemporary chronicles record that fire frequently devastated towns and cities whose buildings were largely constructed from wood; and the blazing bulk of a large church roof could wreak great damage even to its stone walls. A stone vault, on the other hand, could offer considerable protection.

The cathedral builders were also motivated by spiritual considerations. The place of God should be better than all other buildings in every sense – it should be bigger, more beautiful, stronger and more impressive, than everything else around it – and a stone vault over the entire building would achieve this. However, to span a large roof expanse, such as that of a cathedral, was a difficult feat, and to realize these functional and symbolic ideals in stone, real practical problems had to be overcome.

To span a space with wood, a number of timber beams are placed across it at regular intervals. If the space is to be vaulted, each flat beam is replaced by a system of shorter bridging beams. A stone vault, however, is formed by a series of arches built from blocks of stone. The arches are built on (or sprung from) imposts (horizontal mouldings) which in turn rest on columns (the whole construction being called a pier) or supporting walls. The arches themselves are constructed with voussoirs (wedge-shaped blocks of stone) which under pressure exert thrust sideways, thereby holding each other in place. Whereas the wooden beam transmits a simple vertical thrust, the stone arch creates an oblique one which, as the span increases in width, becomes more difficult to counterbalance. The builders of Durham were to invent an ingenious solution for this problem.

The layout of the cathedral

The cruciform plan of Durham's Norman cathedral is of a type usually adopted for a Benedictine church (this was of course a church which served a Benedictine Order, as well as a great cathedral). It has a central nave divided into eight bays and an aisle on each side; transepts run to the north and south, each with its own eastern aisle containing three bays; the choir has five bays. The bay design has three storeys. At ground level is the arcade, a series of arches supported by piers running down each side of the nave, the piers marking off the bays. The middle storey at the level of the side aisle roof is called the triforium. At this level each bay has an arch, and within each arch there are generally two smaller arches supported by shafts. There is a passage or walkway which runs above the side aisles at this level. The upper storey is called the clerestory, and there is a window in each bay at this level. The apse, which stood originally at the eastern end of the cathedral, was flanked by aisles which were also concluded at their eastern ends by smaller apses. A central tower was positioned over the junction of nave and transepts, and a further pair of towers at the western end of the nave.

This Norman structure has survived largely intact for over eight centuries, having lost only the apses, which were removed in the thirteenth century to create space for the Transept of the Nine Altars, and the low central tower which became unsafe and had to be rebuilt in the fifteenth century.

The body of the church was planned so that the nave was roughly twice the width of the side aisles, which were subdivided into square bays. The nave arches spring from huge compound piers which are alternated with visually gentler cylindrical piers. The system of alternating piers is Lombardic, but was not generally adopted by Norman builders (though it was used at the abbey of Jumiéges).

The Durham forms of arch ordering and compound piers also had their roots in the innovations of the Lombards. The arches are built in a series of stepped semi-circles, which allowed relatively small voussoirs to be used. The small size of the voussoirs was a great advantage because they could be handled easily by one or two men, thus saving on labour and costs. The arch construction was elegant in its simplicity: the innermost order of voussoirs was constructed first, the next order was laid upon it so as to partially project, and the process was repeated until the required thickness was reached. This form of arch in turn

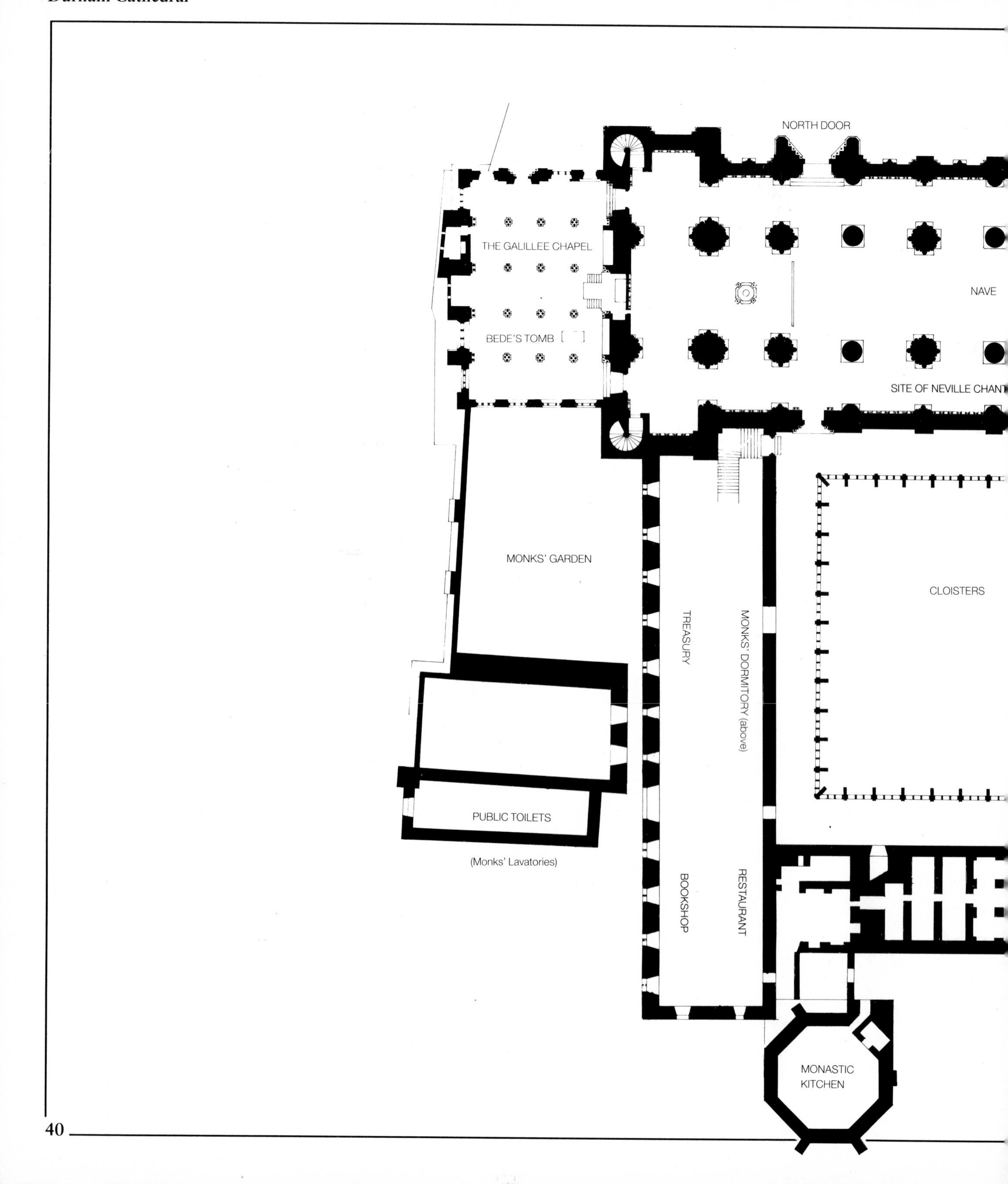
NORTH DOOR
THE GALILLEE CHAPEL
NAVE
BEDE'S TOMB
SITE OF NEVILLE CHANT
MONKS' GARDEN
CLOISTERS
TREASURY
MONKS' DORMITORY (above)
PUBLIC TOILETS
(Monks' Lavatories)
BOOKSHOP
RESTAURANT
MONASTIC
KITCHEN

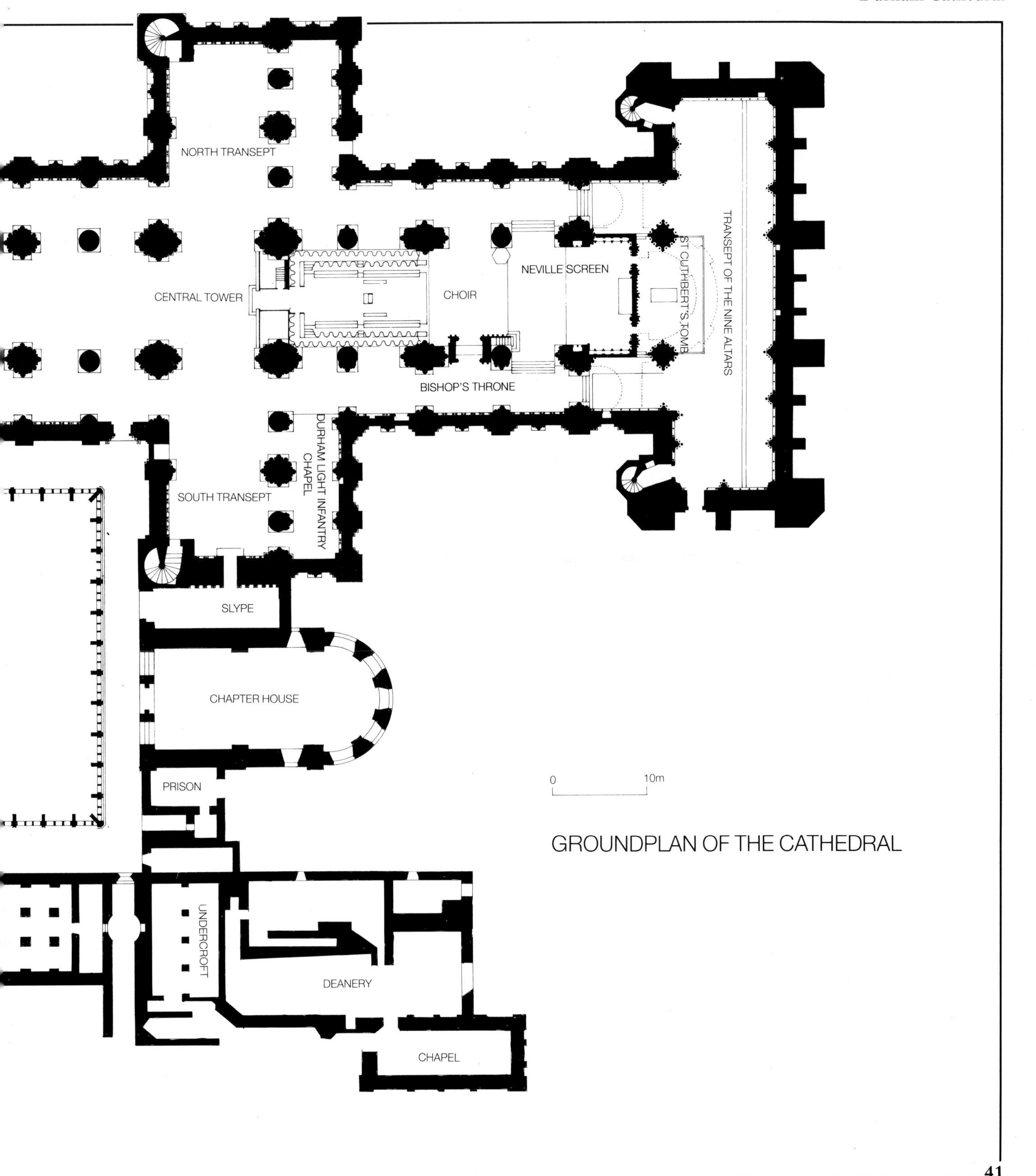

GROUNDPLAN OF THE CATHEDRAL

affected the form of the compound piers supporting it: each step of the arch was provided with a similarly projecting component in the pier which carried it, creating a series of projections and recesses in the structure of the pier which correspond to the stepped orders of the arch. Such articulation of pier and arch was later developed into a significant feature of Gothic architecture.

The development of the vaulting system

The conventional plan of Durham Cathedral belies a structural system that marked a major step forward in architectural engineering, and which was in advance of anything hitherto attempted in either Britain or France. Not only did the Norman masons introduce the use of diagonal ribs to support the stone vaulting; through their invention of the flying buttress they overcame the problem of the oblique thrust of the stone arch.

One of the prime concerns of the builders of Durham when they designed the vaulting system was the need to strengthen the inherently weak groin vault which was normally employed by the builders of the period (including the Lombards). The groin vault is formed by two simple barrel vaults which intersect at right angles, forming four curving triangular surfaces. The curved lines created at these intersections are called groins and the surfaces between them are called cells. At Durham the masons developed a revolutionary system of supporting stone ribs for the vaulting. They built a pair of stone ribs (or arches), positioned diagonally across a bay to make a four-cell framework, which could then be infilled with masonry to create the vault. Thus the masons erected the earliest example of the quadripartite vault in Britain.

Though advanced for its time, this early quadripartite vault, which was probably used in the original choir, was crude in form. Elliptic in shape, the diagonal ribs proved to be as weak a mode of vaulting as the plain groin vault. However, as the masons moved through the building they discovered that by changing the nature of the curve of the rib to form a semi-circle they could strengthen it. To maintain a level ridge along the roof line, they had to spring the two diagonal ribs in a pair from different levels, which destroyed the harmony of the form.

The problem which the masons then had to solve was how to make a quadripartite vault with arches that could all be sprung from the same

ABOVE LEFT AND RIGHT Vaulting in the south transept, showing the triforium level with paired chamber openings of differing designs. To either side, springing from compound piers, are transverse arches between which are double or quadripartite vaults. To the right are the twinned two-light, plain-glazed windows of the central tower, which have perpendicular tracery.

BELOW LEFT The star-shaped symmetry of the vaulting in the fifteenth-century central tower lantern is formed by four principal ribs. These spring from columns that are flanked by windows occurring in four identical pairs on the sides of the tower. Tiercerons and liernes (secondary and tertiary ribs) spring from single columns positioned in each of the four corners of the tower.

BELOW RIGHT An unusual view from the clerestory gallery in the easternmost bay of the nave, looking down towards the crossing. It shows the fine detail on the ribs of the quadripartite vaulting springing from the major compound piers of the crossing. To the left the relatively simple column which flanks the clerestory opening is lit from behind by a window.

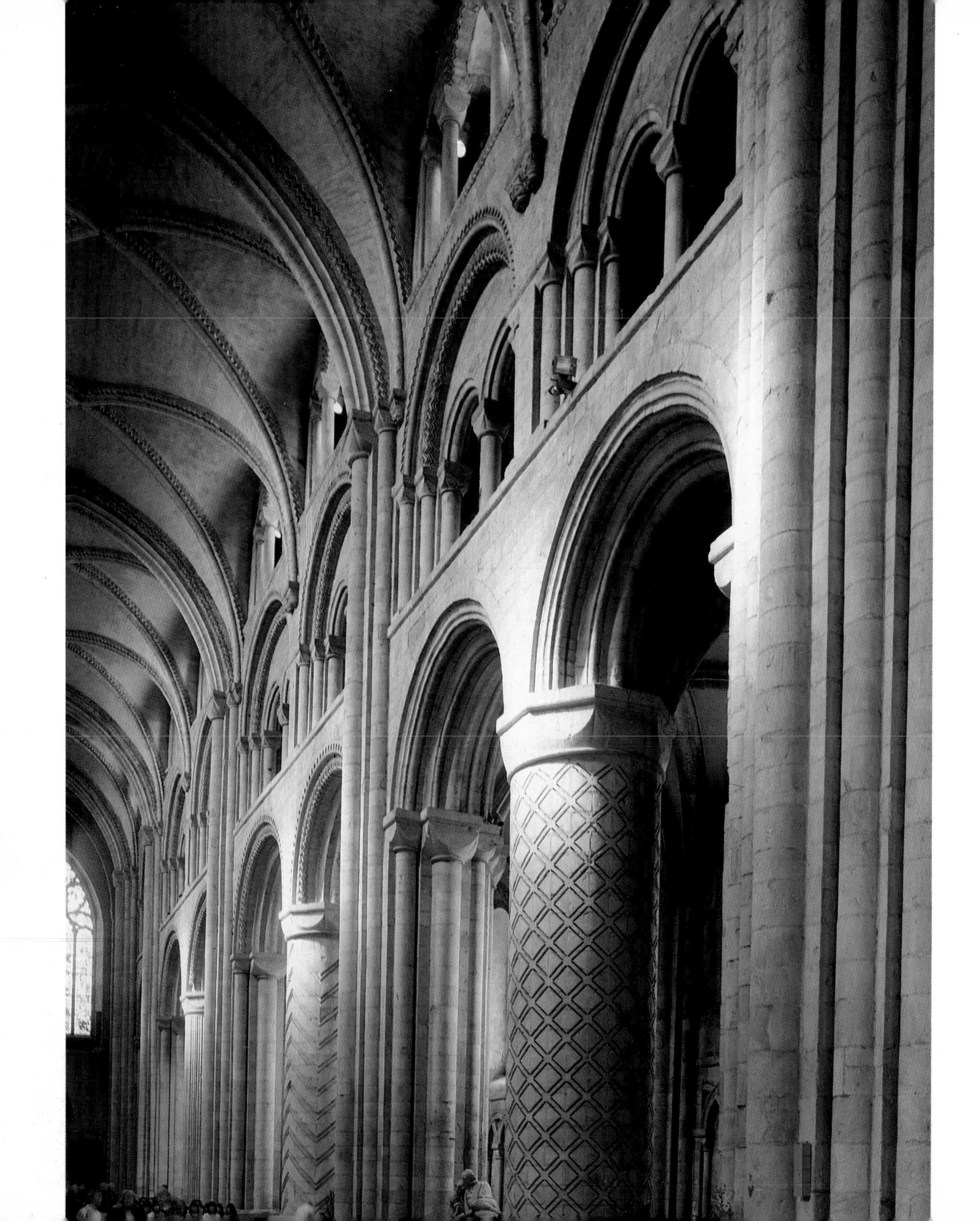

OPPOSITE The vertical qualities of the nave are emphasized by the flute, chevron and reticulated pier designs together with the powerful compound piers which reach up through the triforium level to provide a firm support for the pointed transverse arches.

OVERLEAF LEFT Looking west down the length of the nave there is an excellent view of the fourteenth-century west window. The nave is flanked by alternating massive compound and cylindrical piers; the latter are decorated with carved chevron and reticulated patterns. Above them is the arched opening of the triforium level built by the Normans to contain the structurally important flying buttresses and protect them from the harsh weather conditions experienced in the north of England. Each opening has two sub-arches, their division supported by a slender shaft.

OVERLEAF RIGHT This eastern view of the nave, taken from the triforium level, is interrupted first by a seventeenth-century font cover, and then by an alabaster and marble choir screen which was erected by Sir Gilbert Scott in 1876. The most powerful elements in this view, however, are the huge piers which run down either side of the nave. Rising from the massive compound piers are vaulting shafts, from which spring pointed transverse arches. Between these arches are pairs of diagonally crossing arches. The clerestory level with its single window in each bay is just visible above the triforium arches.

level. In the nave, they had an additional problem to contend with, and that was the shape of the bays. The body of the cathedral had been prepared in the Lombardic tradition, which provided square bays for vaulting. However, square bays created an enormous span for the innovative diagonal ribs, and oblong bays were obviously more expedient. The masons' solution was to create oblong bays from the large square bays by dividing each into a couplet of oblongs, each supporting two pairs of diagonal ribs. The problem of maintaining the heights and levels was greatly complicated by the use of oblong bays, because for the three spans involved, three different height calculations were required. The solution reached for this combination of problems represented yet another extremely important architectural innovation. The masons of Durham employed a rounded arch only for a diagonal span and then, in order to use supporting ribs whilst simultaneously maintaining levels and in particular a flat ridge along the line of the roof, they introduced the use of the pointed arch for the other spans. In this form of arch, the curves each have a radius equal to the span. The pointed arch is created by removing the keystone, which has the added advantage of lessening the sideways pressure exerted by the arch, because it is the keystone which exerts the greatest pressure.

The masons of Durham, by their ingenious use of diagonally ribbed vaults, had fulfilled the aims of the church builders of Europe: they had surmounted their entire structure with a roof of stone. Their inventions did, however, cause them further difficulties. Most importantly, the masons had to ensure that the enormous weight of the great vaulted roof remained stable. For the aisles this was a relatively simple matter of shoring up the outside walls with buttresses. The high vault over the choir and nave, however, produced much greater thrusts, and to contend with these the masons needed some sort of device to transmit the thrust from the ribs of the vault through the upper walls and down to the ground, without making the piers and walls excessively thick. Two different solutions were reached.

For the choir, strong semi-circular arches were built in the triforium chamber, although in time these proved to be incorrectly positioned; they failed to abut the clerestory wall high enough to take the thrust of the vault and had to be rebuilt about a century later.

The solution employed for the nave came to be known as the flying buttress. Its introduction, usually credited to the builders of Durham

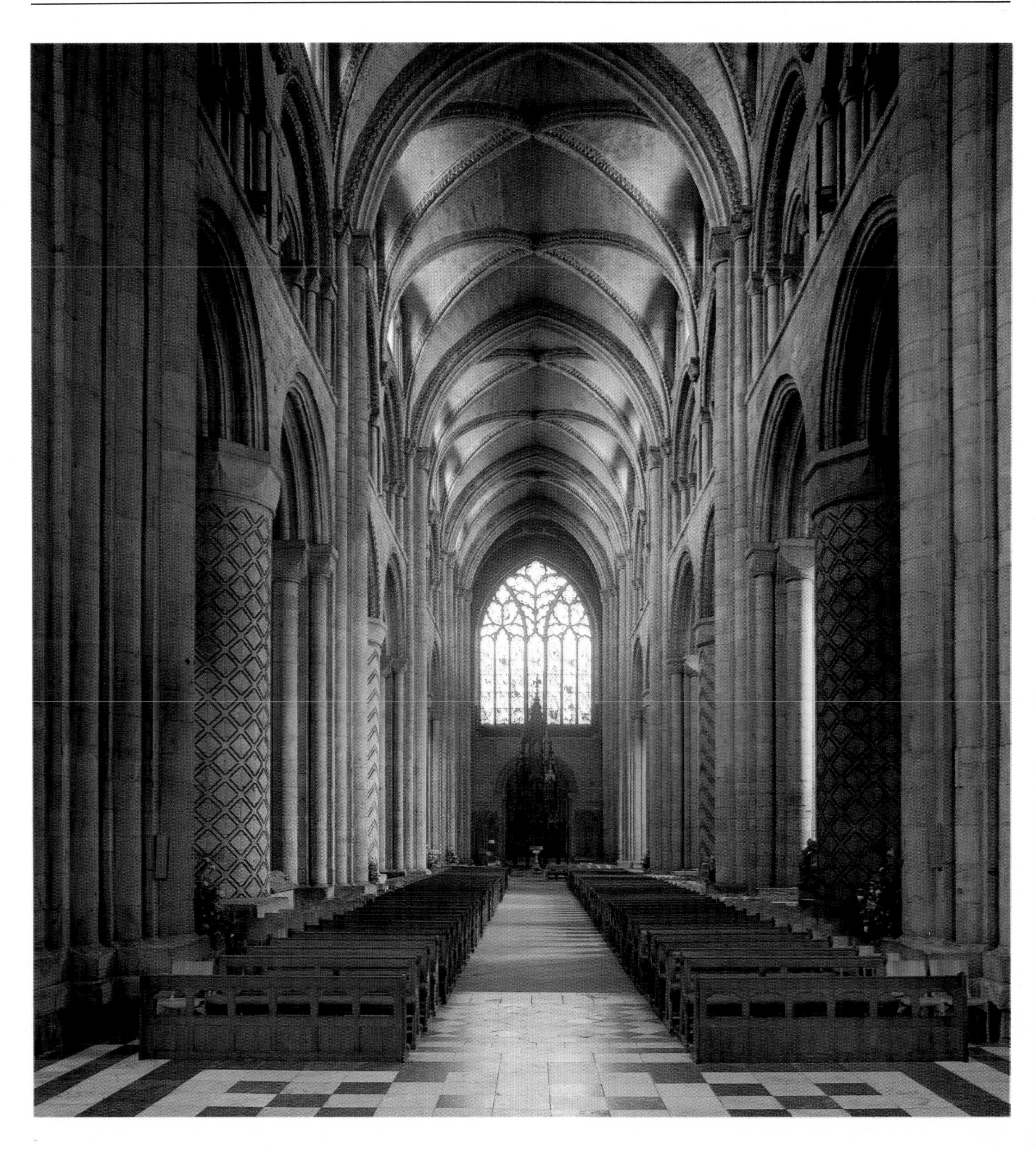

ABOVE LEFT The triforium arch is divided into two bays between the compound columns, while the clerestory level has central openings springing from free-standing columns with a minor arch on either side. Light from the clerestory windows illuminates the decoration on the ribbed vaulting system. The nave vaulting has alternate pointed arches on compound piers, with double quadripartite vaults between them.

ABOVE RIGHT On either side of the central arch which springs from the middle of the compound piers are a pair of intersecting arches; one pair has a zigzag design while the other has been left plain. They are located in the south aisle.

BELOW These flying buttresses over the south nave aisle cannot be seen by the general public, but they are one of the most important architectural details in the cathedral. For the nave vaults, quadrant arches were built underneath the triforium chamber roof to form flying buttresses. These largely hidden buttresses strengthen the clerestory wall and shore up the high nave vault by transmitting its sideways thrust over the side aisles to the outer walls, which are in turn made firm by wall buttresses. The invention of the flying buttress is usually accredited to the masons of Durham Cathedral.

(see, for example, Alec Clifton-Taylor's *The Cathedrals of England*), proved to be a major advance in building design. The flying buttress is an arch or part-arch built against and at right angles to the outside of the upper part of the nave walls. It transfers the sideways thrust of the nave vaults from the top of these walls to the outer walls, which are themselves buttressed to secure the side-aisle vaults as well. The flying buttresses, which at Durham are hidden from general view under the sloping triforium roofs (they can be seen by standing in the triforium) very effectively stabilize the forces at work in the structure and render the clerestory secure.

Decoration within the cathedral

Despite the technical inventiveness of the masons in avoiding the need for hugely thick walls and piers in this way, the structure does retain a quality of massiveness. Indeed, internally, it is not the special qualities of the vaulting and buttresses which make the initial and most lasting impression, but rather the solidity of the masonry. The compound piers, which alternate with circular ones, measure some 16 feet in width in the choir. Those in the nave are less bulky, the circular piers being around 6½ feet in diameter. The circular piers, which were all begun in 1093, are particularly striking as they are decorated with carved channelling. In the nave three patterns are used: chevron, reticulated, and vertical flutings; on the four choir piers and three of the four transept piers a spiral pattern is used. The southernmost transept pier has chevron patterning. This rich decoration was prefabricated; the piers were carefully carved in sections and then assembled on site.

During the Romanesque period piers often carried painted decorations (outstanding examples may be found in Notre Dame la Grande at Poitiers), but such carved decoration was much less common. Furthermore, because most of the patterned piers are organized in a symmetrical plan, there has been speculation as to whether their purpose was purely decorative, or whether the patterns have some symbolic function linked to their proximity to altars, shrines and other sanctified areas within the church. The latter argument is supported by comparative studies of similar pier decoration, particularly in the Netherlands, such as the decorated piers of the crypts of St Peter at Utrecht and St Lebuin at Daventer. However, the significance of the decoration remains equivocal, and at best its symbolism is blurred.

At least part of the cathedral was decorated with red and black paintwork. A small portion has survived the centuries and can still be seen on the south arcading. In addition, there were probably many colourful murals such as the one found recently in the deanery. Although in poor condition, its paint very badly flaked and the image itself scrawled over, it is a poignant indication of the building's former appearance. The scenes depicted have been identified as the annunciation, the nativity, the resurrection, and the ascension, illustrating a medieval hymn to the Virgin, circa 1470. More wall paintings have survived in the Galilee Chapel (see page 92) including a crucifixion and two figures that are thought to represent St Cuthbert and King Oswald. The combination of richly coloured murals, highly decorated screens and piers, bejewelled shrines and 'most fyne colored glas' (*Rites of Durham*), would have created a sense of overwhelming spectacle to the local people, while offering a powerful statement about the status of the palatinate to visiting dignitaries.

Quickly built, the cathedral was soon to be altered and added to. The originator of much late twelfth century building work was Bishop Hugh of Le Puiset. He was the son of Hugh of Le Puiset III, Viscount of Chartres, and Agnes, granddaughter of William the Conqueror. Other powerful family connections included Henry of Blois, the Bishop of Winchester. It was probably under his patronage that Le Puiset came to England, at the age of 14, to take up the post of archdeacon of Winchester. He rose through the ecclesiastical power structure to be enthroned at Durham in 1154.

The Galilee Chapel

In 1175, under the rule of Bishop Hugh of Le Puiset, the Norman apses were demolished, and construction began on a new chapel just behind the shrine of St Cuthbert. It is generally thought that the new chapel was originally planned as a lady chapel. However, work did not progress very well as cracks kept appearing in the fresh masonry, and it was said that St Cuthbert was showing his displeasure at the siting of a lady chapel so near to his shrine. Until this time women had been restricted to the west end of the nave, where a line of blue-black marble set into the floor marks the point beyond which they were not allowed

The ribbed vault of the choir was rebuilt in the latter part of the thirteenth century after the earlier Norman vaulting system was found to be unstable. Viewed here from the high altar, Bishop Hatfield's chantry (1365-75) can be seen on the left-hand side. It consists of a carved arch over which a bishop's throne is reached by means of a short flight of steps. The throne is backed by a stone screen and the whole composition, which is largely perpendicular in style, is tipped with golden decorations. Under the arch is Hatfield's tomb, upon which is an alabaster effigy. Further west are mid-seventeenth-century choir stalls.

ABOVE Sumptuously decorated, picked out in gold and prominently situated in the choir, this tomb of Bishop Thomas Hatfield is a telling memorial to a powerful man. It was built circa 1365-75, and is considered by some to be the finest monument in the cathedral.

BELOW The blank arcading of the south nave aisle was once decorated with wall paintings. Small sections of a reticulated pattern and a daisy-like design have survived, and in one bay restoration gives an idea of the aisle's former appearance.

to pass. The site of the lady chapel was duly moved by Bishop Le Puiset to an area just outside the west door. The description of a contemporary reçorder, and possible eyewitness to the event, Geoffry of Coldingham, states, 'Bishop Hugh began to construct an aisle at the east end of the church. . . however, although employing the most skilful masons at great expense there were as many starts as masters, as whenever the walls were built to any height, great cracks appeared in them. . . which was thought to indicate to him that God and his servant Cuthbert disapproved. The work was stopped and transferred to the west, where women would be allowed to enter; so those who had not had access to the secret and holy places might gain solace from the contemplation of them' [Script Tres.II. translated by R. Halsey].

The new site at the west front was cramped because the escarpment on which the cathedral is perched falls away steeply at this point. Structurally, it presented greater building problems than had the original eastern site, and in addition, expensive materials provided for the eastern site had to be adapted to meet its limitations. The new siting also effectively closed the cathedral on its western side, blocking the great west door and rendering it obsolete as the main entrance. Nevertheless, the architecture is a delight. Forty-eight feet long and 75 feet wide, the space became known as the Galilee Chapel, its name a reference to Jesus telling the disciples that he would go before them to Galilee. [Galilee is the term sometimes applied to the area of a church where regular Sunday processions end – it could, for example, mark an exit, as with the Galilee porches at both Ely and Lincoln cathedrals.]

The Galilee Chapel had three functions: as a place of worship for women, who were allowed little other access into the main body of the cathedral; as a processional space; and as an ecclesiastical court. This variety of purpose, together with the unusual topography of the cramped rock-top site, and the need to use the resources which had been provided for the eastern site, combined to affect substantially the design of this west end extension to the cathedral.

The space within the Galilee is divided into five equal aisles by arcades, each of which has four bays, providing a good open space for the bishop's court. The dominant great west door was incorporated into the design of the Chapel by flanking it with buttresses, and aligning piers with it. From slim cluster-piers spring semi-circular arches edged with a rhythmic, carved, chevron pattern. Each pier has two shafts of

Purbeck marble and two more of sandstone (which date either from the same period or possibly from the fifteenth century). Purbeck marble was rarely used in the north of England, though it was employed around 1175 in the reconstruction of the choir of Canterbury Cathedral, and Bishop Le Puiset probably saw it used by his uncle, Bishop Henry of Blois, at Winchester. The capitals are not marble, but are made from freestone carved with a waterleaf motif. Similar carvings can be found in York, in both the Minster and St Mary's Abbey, and it is thought that craftsmen from Yorkshire may have done the carvings at Durham. Unusually for the time, the names of two masons involved with the Galilee – Richard and William – were recorded. It is possible that Richard was the Bishop's master-mason or architect, for he was a man of some wealth and property.

The contrast between the original Norman building and the later Galilee extension is marked. While the former is massive, the latter has an intrinsic grace which is mainly due to the slender proportions of the piers. The roof of the Galilee has only a low timber roof, which may reflect an unwillingness to be adventurous after the structural problems experienced on the original eastern site. The lowness of the roof was also functional, as it allows light into the west end of the nave and aisles through the large west window. The exterior of the roof dates mainly from Cardinal Langley's time (1428-35), with additions by Wyatt (*c.* 1790) and Scott (1865-68) (see Chapter 4). Langley was also responsible for the four great buttresses which shore up the west front of the Galilee (which nevertheless still leans outwards), and he also added the three central windows. The south wall was reconstructed in the early fourteenth century, along with part of the north wall.

The Transept of the Nine Altars

After the erection of the Galilee came the construction of a second transept, the Transept of the Nine Altars, at the eastern end of the cathedral on the very ground which had been rejected for the construction of a Lady Chapel.

Additional space and better access were needed for the ever-increasing number of pilgrims and for the general congregation in those parts of the cathedral that housed devotional altars and the all-important, income-generating relics. The shrine of St Cuthbert, which brought the cathedral huge revenues, presented particular problems as

RIGHT The lightness and prettiness of the twelfth-century Galilee Chapel offers a real contrast to the clean-lined massiveness which characterizes the powerful nave and transepts. Though late Norman in style, the Galilee has a number of transitional qualities such as flattened attic bases, waterleaf capitals and keeled arch mouldings. Its nave is divided into four bays and is flanked by inner and outer aisles. There are twelve detached Purbeck marble shafts, each topped by a decorated waterleaf capital. From the capitals spring arches that are strikingly patterned with a sharp zigzag design.

BELOW The delicate arches, waterleaf capitals and slim shafts of the Galilee, looking east, are dappled with sunlight which enters through windows inserted during the centuries following the chapel's construction. They undoubtedly make for a much brighter space than that created by Bishop Hugh of Le Puiset's builders.

From the outside, the twelfth-century Galilee Chapel has a strange relationship with the main body of the cathedral, as its relatively small proportions are at odds with the massive quality of the west end. The chapel, which occupies a very tight site on the edge of the precipe, was shored up with buttresses during the fifteenth century.

it was very poorly positioned, tucked away in an apse behind the high altar. The throngs of pilgrims seeking a glimpse of the holy relic had to violate the sanctuary area of the choir, thus reducing its status within the church. It was thought that a second transept would solve the problem; it would contain plenty of altars, provide extra space for large gatherings, and have sufficient room to allow a regulated flow of pilgrims. It would also provide a new home for the remains of St Cuthbert (the precedent for re-siting precious saints' remains had been set at York Minster, where Archbishop Roger of Pont l'Eveque, who was well-known to Bishop Le Puiset, was responsible for re-building the chancel in order to relocate the Minster's relics).

To raise money for the new transept, numerous indulgences were granted to patrons willing to make sizeable contributions to the building fund, not only by the Bishop of Durham, but also by other bishops supporting the cause. For example, Hugh Northwold, Bishop of Ely, offered 30 days remission to those who would help fund the new vaulted space over the tomb of St Cuthbert at Durham.

The ground available at Durham for an extension to the cathedral was limited. Some transverse design to the east of the site seemed topographically most appropriate, as it would provide the maximum ground area, although a smaller extension could have been sited to form a second cruciform. The lie of the land ruled out the possibility of adapting the plan employed at Winchester Cathedral, another Benedictine house which had, like Durham, organisational considerations associated with its relics. The length of Winchester, which at 556 feet is the longest Gothic church in Europe, prevented it being chosen as a model for Durham, where the site fell away too steeply at the eastern end to allow any substantial eastward extension to its nave.

Instead the powers at Durham looked to Fountains Abbey in Yorkshire for a solution to the problem of lack of space. There, a second eastern transept had been added between 1203 and 1247 to accommodate a greatly increased community of monks. That the Benedictine house of Durham should look to the Cistercian monastery of Fountains is unusual and intriguing since they were quite separate Orders not given to employing each others' systems.

In 1242, work on the Transept of the Nine Altars began. The juxtaposition of the new transept with the existing Norman choir was a difficult one, as the fall of the land forced the new transept to be built on a level about 3 feet lower than that of the choir. Proportionally, however, there were great advantages to be obtained from the extra height of the transept, which emphasized the vertical structure, and resulted in the extension being built in what was to become the Early English style. It is a mighty extension some 120 feet from north to south. Elegant cluster piers with slender shafts made from Frosterly marble (the local substitute for the expensive Purbeck marble) divide the bays. There are graceful blind arcades, in the form of a series of trefoiled arches applied to the walls, forming a dado below a narrow, window-level wall passage. Yet most striking of all is the preoccupation of the design with the stability of the masonry. The walls, which are some 7 feet thick, are shored by 4 feet 6 inch buttresses, but those which flank the central bay are massive, projecting about 10 feet outwards. In addition, the four corners of the transept are buttressed with hefty corner turrets and there are substantial responds, or half-piers, bonded into the wall. Such a preoccupation with stability is understandable on this eastern site, given the failure of the earlier chapel.

The vaulting system is interesting for its faults. The outer bays are quadripartite, but for two of the inner bays it seems that, having taken the dimensions for his vaults from those of the Nine Altars Transept at Fountains Abbey, the designer only discovered when building work was well advanced that the proportions of the nave and aisle at Fountains are quite different from those at Durham. Thus, the vaulting at Durham became mismatched. The mason was forced to make the transverse arch cut directly across the quadripartite vaulting system, springing it from the pier where the transept meets the wall of the outer choir aisle. This rather make-do solution is clearly visible – absolutely no attempt was made to hide or disguise it.

The builder who supervised its construction was 'Magister Riccardus de Farinham architector novae fabricae Dunelm'. Interestingly, one of the carved heads on the wall of the arcading is thought to be a likeness of this master-mason. He may have been a relative of Nicholas of Farnham who was, at the time, Bishop of Durham. A second mason is recorded, this time by an inscription on a buttress of the eastern wall – 'Posuit hanc petram Thomas Moises'.

Once more, St Cuthbert was moved, this time to a raised platform which projected from the choir into the new Transept of the Nine

OPPOSITE A dramatic view along the recently restored roof of the choir to the Transept of the Nine Altars, whose buttressed corners are topped with nineteenth-century pinnacles. Terraced houses (many now with Georgian façades) surround the cathedral and once formed the medieval town, while in the distance spreads the modern city.

OVERLEAF The east side of the Transept of the Nine Altars is divided into nine bays, each separated by large compound responds. In each bay is a tall lancet and at sill level a narrow wall-passage runs through the thickness of the responds. A further passage runs at high level. Here, the view north is dominated by a large Gothic window that has fine intersecting tracery, beneath which is blank arcading.

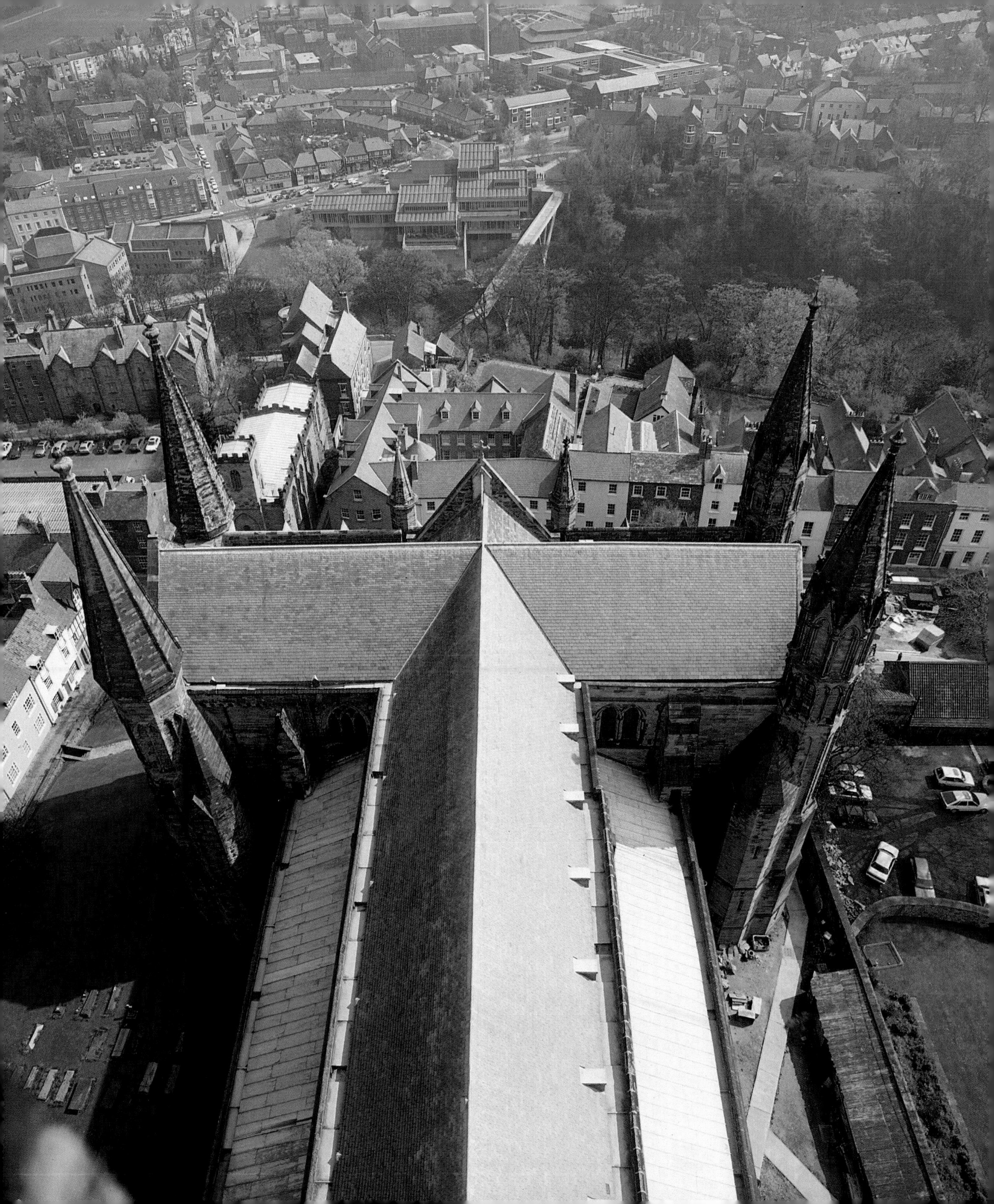

Altars. The new shrine was said to be 'exalted with most curious workmanship, of fine and costly green marble all limned and gilted with gold, having four seats convenient underneath, for the pilgrims or lame men sitting on their knees to lean and rest on in the time of their devout offerings and fervent prayers to God and holy St Cuthbert for his miraculous relief and succour' [*Rites of Durham*].

Completion of the medieval building

Including the eastern Nine Altars Transept and the Galilee Chapel, the total length of Durham Cathedral is 469 feet 6 inches. Its size met the needs of the adjacent monastery for the next two and a half centuries. In the fourteenth century, the sanctuary was rejuvenated by the addition of the Neville Screen. Work on the screen, which was a gift from John, Lord Neville of Raby, began in 1372. It was chiselled from Caen stone by masons in London who were highly skilled in the Perpendicular Gothic style. Once carved, the screen had to be carefully transported to Durham, divided into sections which were packed in large trunks. These were sent by sea to Newcastle, and thereafter by cart to Durham. Once erected in the sanctuary, the screen would have impressed the lay folk and clergy alike. It was filled with some 107 images of saints and martyrs, each carved and coloured by the alabaster craftsmen of Nottingham.

No further substantial building work was undertaken in the main body of the cathedral, except to open up a number of walls to provide new windows. These included the great west window of the nave (1341–1374 – but since replaced). In the fifteenth century, a *Te Deum* window in the south transept and a Perpendicular window in the west wall of the Galilee Chapel were introduced. Other building work was confined to restoration of the Galilee Chapel, which was in need of particular attention. In 1428 repair work began on its roof and pier shafts and, between two of the powerful new buttresses constructed to shore up its walls, Cardinal Thomas Langley inserted a small vestry.

In 1429, while the Galilee was still being restored, there was a tremendous storm, during which the wooden belfry of the Norman central tower was struck by lightning and set ablaze, causing great damage to lower stonework and leaving the tower very unstable. Twenty-six years passed before its highly dangerous state made repairs unavoidable, and in 1455 work began to rebuild the section of the

The task of joining the Transept of the Nine Altars onto the existing choir was fraught with problems for the Norman masons. Working on a site substantially lower than that used for the earlier building, they had to make a number of compromises, as can be seen in this detail of the sexpartite vaulting system. Clearly, a construction error was made resulting in the diagonal ribs failing to cross at the centre of the transverse arch.

tower which projected above the roof level of the cathedral. The new tower, 218 feet high, was built in two stages, the first part being completed in 1474. The final topping off with a new belfry was not finished until the end of the century.

The reconstruction of the tower marked the end of medieval building work at Durham, and along with the surviving twin Norman towers, it completed the cathedral's distinctive skyline, which so conspicuously and so completely dominates its surroundings and sends out commanding signals of power and subjugation.

3 Monastic and Other Buildings

Now lawned, the cathedral garth was once the site of the monks' sink, the remains of which (incorrectly positioned) can be seen in the centre. Around the garth are the cloisters, which have lost their glazing, and rising high above the cloisters is the great central tower.

The mighty cathedral of Durham does not stand alone. It shares its windy hilltop site with the Norman castle and, sandwiched between the two, Palace Green (formerly known as 'Place Green') which is today a diligently shorn, though rather bland, piece of lawn. Palace Green once belonged to the bishops, who ruled from their fortress stronghold within the castle's outer walls; now it is the visual point of overlap for castle, university and cathedral. Until the twelfth century the space was covered with a huddle of houses, but they were thought to be a serious fire hazard, and were undesirable in such close proximity to the cathedral. They were demolished, and the Green became encircled by buildings historically connected first with the church and the castle, and latterly with the university.

Today the north side of Palace Green is edged by the castle, which is no longer an imposing stronghold but a friendly university building and tourist attraction. To the east stand a row of early seventeenth-century almshouses which now contain a small restaurant. Along the west side, the building nearest to the castle gate dates from 1450 and was once Bishop Robert Neville's exchequer, but now contains part of the university library. Next to it stands the library which was founded by Bishop Cosin in 1669, and a little further along is a small passage, aptly named Windy Gap, beside which is the early nineteenth-century Diocesan Registry and the university Music Department, housed in what was the Dean and Chapter's grammar school built in 1661. All in all, Palace Green is an area which well demonstrates the interlinking of the cathedral with other concerns of Durham through the ever changing uses of the component architecture.

To the south of the main body of the cathedral, there is another substantial complex of associated buildings. The cathedral was both a symbolic focus of power dominating a whole region of northern England and a chapel for the community of Benedictine monks; and, as such, it needed a substantial support mechanism to maintain, administer and protect it. Many of the servicing tasks were carried out by the monks themselves, who needed somewhere to live and work near the cathedral. In fact, the monastic buildings abut the cathedral, underlining their integrated working relationship.

The cloisters

The cloisters and other monastic buildings are arranged around a garth

ABOVE AND LEFT The north cloister, now empty apart from a few benches, was formerly the monks' scriptorium. Individual carrels once divided the walkway into small sections. Close inspection of the walls reveals peg marks indicating the position of the study chambers and storage cupboards. The fifteenth-century timber ceiling is decorated with shields and bosses which were made in 1409-19.

RIGHT The door at the far end of the east cloister leads into the south nave aisle, one of the two entries into the monastery from the cathedral.

The three-light, unglazed cloister windows date from 1763-77 and are part of the substantial rebuilding work undertaken in the cathedral during the late eighteenth century. Beyond them, in the garth, stands a modern wooden statue of St Cuthbert. It was made by Durham sculptor Fenwick Lawson, who carved it from the trunk of a large elm tree which once stood on the north side of the cathedral. In the background are the triforium and clerestory levels of the south transept.

(the open area in the middle of the cloisters) situated off the south aisle wall of the cathedral. They are reached through doorways either into the west walkway or the east walkway. Now unglazed and very draughty, the cloisters once provided the monks with a sheltered communal area, warmed by the sun, in which to carry out a variety of activities, while the rooms leading off were associated with particular functions. The layout of the approximately 145 square foot garth and surrounding buildings is Norman, and the garth contains one of the community's two wells. Today the garth contains a centrally positioned basin (originally sited further to the south–west) which was once part of the monks lavatorium. Early cloister sinks tended to be round or polygonal and often had small spouts which poured water into individual bowls. It is likely that the first sink at Durham was of this kind, but it was later replaced (probably during an extension of the washing facilities) by an octagonally shaped one housed in a round building topped by a dovecote which was located near to the refectory. The custom of washing hands originated in the Bible (the disciples of Jesus were accused by the Pharisees of transgressing the law by failing to wash their hands before they broke bread), and by medieval times it had become vested with symbolic meaning. It is probable that the monks of Durham engaged in some form of ritualistic washing – perhaps washing their hands before entering the cathedral. Bathing was, however, a different matter, for it seems that washing of the whole body was an activity largely reserved for the sick, who would have been following strict medical advice in what was regarded as a highly risky venture.

The empty cloistered walks, which today offer little temptation to linger, were once a hive of activity, popular with the monks as a pleasant place to read, meditate and study. The north walkway, known as the scriptorium, was divided by timber screens into carrels (small studies) to provide some privacy, while the west walkway was used as a school for novices. The east and south cloisters were, among other things, the areas where the ritualized tradition of washing the feet of the poor took place each year on Maundy Thursday. The rite was observed and recorded by Simeon of Durham:

> 'dyd washe the poore men's feete with his own hands and dryd them with a towell and kissed the feete himselfe, which being done, he did verie liberally bestow [?] in money of everye one of

The door in the north-east corner of the cloister leads into the south nave aisle. Dating from Bishop Le Puiset's time, it has three orders of shafts, each topped with a scalloped or waterleaf capital. However, its most striking feature is the succession of recessed arch borders which are decorated with deeply carved rope, battlement and flower friezes.

them, with seven reade herrings a pice, and did serve them himselfe with drinke and three loaves of bread with certain wafers'

Little remains of the Norman cloisters because they have twice been remodelled and have lost virtually all their original furniture. The first rebuilding was started towards the end of the fourteenth century, financed jointly by Bishop Langley and by the executors of Bishop Skirlaw's estate. Apart from glazing, the work was complete around 1419, but we can only guess at how it looked at this time. The materials used were recorded in the cathedral accounts, and included stone that was quarried at Baxterwood and West Burn (both just a few miles from Durham) and carved under the supervision of master-masons Thomas Mapilton and Thomas Hyndeley. Wood came from the priory manors of Shincliffe and Bearpark, supplemented by supplies from Newcastle and Hartlepool; carpenters John Rasyn and John Wadley were responsible for the woodwork, including the construction of the flat timber ceilings which are, despite nineteenth and twentieth century restoration work, still recognizable. There is, however, little else medieval to see in the cloisters, for during the eighteenth century substantial alterations were made, and it is startling to note that many of the elements – the window tracery, the diagonally flagged flooring – which appear to signify an ancient past, are but two centuries or less old.

Travelling clockwise around the cloisters, the northern side abuts the cathedral, its north wall formed by that of the south aisle. Moving on, the first section of wall enclosing the east cloister walk is the outer façade of the west side of the cathedral's south transept. A slype, or passage, once ran from the east cloister past the end of the south transept, through to the monks cemetery. This narrow barrel-vaulted passage is described in *Rites of Durham* as a place where merchants were allowed to bring their goods for sale. In later years it was used by the monks as a locutorium, or parlour, and is now used as an ante-room for the adjoining chapter house.

The chapter house

The centrally positioned entrance to the chapter house, off the east walkway, is flanked by windows each with continuous mouldings. The doorway itself has a semi-circular head of three orders: the inner is simply moulded, but the outer two have chevron ornamentation

ABOVE LEFT Carved figures on the chapter house north wall are the room's original atlantes (supports). These simple male figures are survivors from the twelfth-century chapter house, where they functioned as entabulature supports.

ABOVE AND RIGHT Capitals offer great opportunities for the stonemason to display his craftsmanship and imagination. These examples are on the doorway to the chapter house. They show a figure and flower motif; a mermaid and serpent; and a floral pattern.

characteristic of the last stage of the nave and therefore suggesting a mid-twelfth century date. The room was used by the prior and monks for meetings; it was the place where they gathered each morning to conduct business associated with the community, and each evening at 5pm for an hour of prayer. The hierarchy of the gathering was clearly expressed in the architecture: a seat was provided at the east end for the Bishop, who was flanked by his most important officers, whilst the monks sat on a stone bench around the edge of the room.

The interior of the chapter house has some architectural interest, but the radical and destructive eighteenth century alterations carried out on the orders of Wyatt (see page 99) have robbed it of atmosphere, and it is disappointing after one has experienced the main body of the church. The original Norman chapter house was 76 feet 6 inches long and 34 feet 6 inches wide with an apsidal east end. A wall arcade ran round the interior of the room, below which was a stone seat. The floor was paved with slabs, many of which covered the burial places of early bishops, including Carileph, Flambard, Rufus and Le Puiset. The subsequent eighteenth-century demolition of the east end reduced the length of the chapter house to 35 feet, making it virtually square in shape, and simultaneously destroyed the whole vaulting system, which was replaced with a new coved roof that cut directly across the five three-light fifteenth-century windows of the west end. The windows on either side of the west doorway were blocked and the walls were covered with lath and plaster. The eighteenth century was undoubtedly a time of architectural mutilation and all work on the chapter house since has consisted of a succession of attempts to reconstruct some of its former glory. In 1830, part of the lath and plaster was removed and by the middle of the century it had all been taken down. The wall arcades were restored in 1847, as were the west wall, doorway and window in 1857. Excavations carried out in 1874 uncovered the floor of the original east end. Determination to carry out major restoration on the chapter house was mounting and in 1895–6, C. Hodgson Fowler supervised the work which attempted to resurrect the former appearance of the east end. The room which we now experience is largely a Victorian restoration of the medieval original.

RIGHT The prison, situated to the south of the chapter house, was used to hold minor offenders. The small, windowless cell was well appointed with basin and lavatory. It also once had a food-hatch, but this was blocked up early in its history when a cemetery passage to the south was constructed.

BELOW Some of the most enchanting examples of Durham's stained glass can be found in the chapter house, like this delightful image of a bird. It is one of a number of diamond-shaped, medieval stained glass panels which are arranged on either side of the chapter house door. All are formed from pale yellow and black and are worth close examination.

The interior of the chapter house today consists of two square bays which are rib vaulted, and an apse at the eastern end, reconstructed largely from the late eighteenth-century drawings of John Carter. The ribs of the apse rest on carved corbels (projecting blocks) whose decorative work includes the use of atlantes (male figures used as pillars), the originals of which did survive the demolition work and are now displayed as sculptural objects on the north wall. Running along the walls are arcades formed by intersecting arches above which is a zigzag frieze. A doorway in the south wall of the chapter house leads to a room, 23 feet long and 12 feet wide, which was used as an ante-chamber to the small prison rooms used for minor offences. From here a further doorway leads to two smaller chambers, one of which contains a food hatch and the other a lavatory. These twin cells are positioned under the flight of stairs which lead to the first of the monks dormitories, the doorway to which is in the cloister.

BELOW The silhouettes in the doorway belong to two canons, as they might have looked had they been Benedictine monks. They are standing just inside the dimly lit passage which leads from the College into the south cloister.

The other monastic buildings

The Norman dormitory occupied the south-east corner of the cloister until the late fourteenth century when, on completion of the new large west dormitory, it became redundant and was pressed into service as part of the prior's dwelling, which clustered behind it outside the cloister plan. The fourteenth century had seen a consolidation of the powers and status of the prior, reflected in his greatly increased lodgings which expanded to include a substantial house, solarium, parlour and servants' quarters. The dormitory was converted into a great hall to complete the impressive complex of the Prior's lodgings. The sub-dormitory, with its two aisles of four-arch arcades, also survives. During the dissolution of the monasteries in the fifteenth century, the present deanery was created in the former prior's mansion, and today this undercroft houses an audio-visual display.

Extending from the east walkway, running alongside the dormitory, is a vaulted passage. A small doorway leads into another early Norman undercroft which was once part of the refectory, and is now occupied by educational display-boards provided to instruct visiting schoolchildren. Originally designed to service the refectory, the eleventh-century undercroft, the oldest of the conventional buildings, was sub-divided into a number of food storage rooms. First comes a narrow barrel-vaulted chamber, then, through a round-arched opening,

ABOVE Dramatically floodlit, the cathedral viewed from Crossgate forms a powerful, almost menacing presence above the town.

RIGHT This monastic kitchen was designed by John Lewyn and built in 1366-74. The central roof design forms an eight-pointed star.

ABOVE Considered by many to be one of the most impressive parts of Durham's monastic complex, the monks' dormitory occupies the entire length of the west range. 194 feet long and 39 feet wide, it was built by Bishop Skirlaw in 1398-1404 as a replacement for an earlier (though not the original) dormitory on the same site. The dominating feature is its solid timber roof, constructed by carpenter Ellis Harpour. Rough-hewn beams span horizontally across the space onto substantial brackets reinforced by diagonal timber ties, terminating on stone corbels. The pitch of the roof is simply achieved by squat timber supports positioned under the purlins. The four purlins and a ridge beam then support the rafters and the boarding under the roof covering. Only the ridge beam has any decoration, limited to a simple notched sequence. The dormitory was converted for use as a library in 1850-56 under architect Philip Charles Hardwick.

BELOW The vaulting in the late fourteenth-century roof of the prior's kitchen forms an eight-pointed star configuration. Ribs cross one another in a one to four and six, two to five and seven, three to six and eight, four to seven and one, five to eight and two, arrangement. This resulted in the creation of a minor inner octagon which once carried a skylight. The stone ribs are infilled with brick, completing a roof which is free from timber and therefore relatively fire resistant – an important consideration in the design of a medieval kitchen.

there is a large groin-vaulted area, some 50 feet by 32 feet. This is divided by stumpy 2 feet 6 inch square piers into three 7 feet 6 inch wide aisles. Despite the vaulting, the ceiling is low, just 7 feet 6 inches. Three further small chambers are located to the west of the main space, each spanned by barrel vaults. Deriving natural light from a series of small round-headed windows, the refectory undercroft is less gloomy than many similar spaces.

The overhead refectory was an altogether different room, described in *Rites of Durham* as, 'a fair large Hall . . . which is finely wainscotted both on the North and Southside thereof, and in the West and neither part . . . there is a fair long bench of hewen stone, Mason work to sitt on which is from the Seller door to the Pantry or Covey door . . .' On ordinary days, the refectory was a large simple eating area, but on special occasions, such as St Cuthbert's Day, it was transformed into a sumptuous feasting place. However, the chronicler's description is virtually the only record of the once great dining-hall because it gradually fell from favour, the monks choosing instead to eat in a small adjoining room known as 'the loft'. In the seventeenth century it became the extensive Dean and Chapter library.

To the south-west of the refectory stands the most exciting of the monastery buildings, the kitchen. Designed by John Lewyn and dating from 1366–74, it is innovative in its structure and delightful in its organization. The space is square with huge fire-places on each wall. Further huge ranges positioned at angles in each corner create an octagonal shape, a deception emphasized by the octagonally shaped, vaulted roof structure. The eight semi-circular ribs each span three sides – one to four and six, two to five and seven, three to six and eight, four to seven and one, five to eight and two – forming a smaller, inner octagon by their lines of intersection. A stone vault would have been an important asset to a medieval kitchen where there was a constant threat from fire, and it would have carried some form of louvred smoke escape. It is now topped by a replica eighteenth century lantern. On the outside the building is bulky and square, the spaces behind the ranges being filled out by the store-rooms.

If the kitchen is the most appealing monastic building by virtue of its imaginative and attractive eight-point-star vault construction, then the west dormitory, by force of its enormous size, is the most impressive. It occupies the full west range of the cloisters and extends some more, jutting beyond the quadrangle into the College, a total of 194 feet long and some 39 feet wide. It was constructed in 1404 on the site of a previous dormitory (though not the earliest dormitory which, as discussed earlier, was on the east side), of which fragments of wall, a Norman doorway and sections of the reredorter (latrines) survive. The latter was a substantial building thought to have been about 68 feet long and 30 feet wide connected to the dormitory by a ground-level passage. Near to it was an underground prison where serious offenders were held secure. Incarceration must have been a miserable fate and a harsh punishment, as the prisoner was held in dark isolation for a year or more, receiving food lowered by a rope.

The dormitory undercroft, which is well preserved, is arranged by short circular piers into a twelve-bay plan. The northern section, the medieval spendement or strong-room, was restored in the 1840s by Anthony Salvin and again in 1971–3 by G. G. Pace. The area formed by the other bays, which was used by the monks as a common-room, was restored, again by Salvin, and has been converted for use by cathedral visitors: a bookshop and restaurant, 1974–5, by Pace; and a treasury, 1977–8, by Curry. The visitors are also serviced by toilets which are sited over the original monastic lavatory.

The large dormitory, dominated by a massive roof constructed from roughly cut oak timbers, is striking in appearance. Its lofty space, reminiscent of a baronial hall, was divided into numerous cubicles which were used as study-bedrooms by the monks. They were arranged in two long rows, down the east and west walls, accessed by a central passage which was paved with, 'fine tyled stone' [*Rites of Durham*]. The room was lit by small straight-headed windows which each serviced two individual cubicles providing the monks with some warmth from whatever sunshine there was. Above these are tall two-light Perpendicular windows which introduced light into the great bulk of the dormitory. The novices slept in the south end, which was considered to be less comfortable, 'having eight chambers on each side. . .not so close nor warm as the others . . .' [*Rites of Durham*]. The monks were supervized by the sub-prior, whose chamber was near the door at the northern end of the dormitory that leads down to the west cloister walkway. All the original fittings have long since disappeared from the dormitory and the room is now used by the Dean and Chapter library for their collection of relatively recent books. Nevertheless,

ABOVE This light, airy room was once the monks' refectory. It was converted for use as a library in the 1680s and today retains its interesting seventeenth-century bookcases. They are designed with the intention of recreating something of the monastic studies, which combined seat, desk and bookcase in a single unit. In this instance the result is elegant, but rather uncomfortable to use. The library holds over 20,000 published items dating from 1501 to around 1800, including some 11,000 dissertations produced in European universities from the sixteenth to the early nineteenth centuries.

BELOW This marble line in the west end floor marked the limit beyond which no woman was allowed to venture. In 1333, Queen Philippa visited Durham with her husband Edward III and, unaware of the prohibition, passed over the line to reach sleeping quarters with the monastery. The monks, keen to uphold their ancient traditions, told the king that St Cuthbert would be displeased by her presence and Queen Philippa was made to leave the cathedral precincts and sleep instead in the castle.

This beautiful panel of glass, known as 'the sacrament of matrimony', is part of the first window in the west wall of the Galilee Chapel. It is thought to date from around 1435. However, although the full window of ten panels contains fragments of medieval glass salvaged from other parts of the cathedral, this section is considered by experts to have some other origin.

when using the underheated library for research or study, perhaps sitting at a desk in a weak pool of sunlight, it is not at all difficult to conjure up images of the monks similarly engaged (and similarly shivering!) at small tables within their cubicles.

Apart from the buildings described, set round the cloister, the cathedral complex contains a number of others. Some are dwellings arranged around the College (Durham's equivalent of a cathedral close), and some were service buildings, such as stables and brewhouses, which are now used as workshops for the cathedral's permanent staff of masons and carpenters. The College, although allowing public access, is an almost secret place tucked away to the south of the refectory. It can be reached by walking from the cloister through a dimly-lit passage, or, from the street, through the gatehouse over which is the tiny St Helen's Chapel. Though the College is of limited architectural interest, it is a very pleasant place through which to wander. Of particular interest are No. 16, which is built on the site of the former chamberlain's exchequer; the terrace of stone prebendal houses built right on the edge of the precipice; the octagonal, Gothic-revival, conduit house; the choir school; and the neatly maintained lawn.

Seeing this attractive area now, it is hard to imagine that during the fifteenth and sixteenth centuries the monastic settlement, along with the cathedral and Durham in general, gradually fell into ruin. By the latter part of the seventeenth century a seemingly endless process of decay had taken hold which saw the castle and the city walls crumble. The area around the cathedral, a circle of roofless and mainly abandoned hovels was squalid; piles of rubbish which had for long been heaved over the city walls were festering; and morale was low. It was a place where the combined problems of fighting, political changes and pestilence had all taken their toll; it had been subject to both great use and great abuse.

4 Use and Abuse

Down to the smallest detail, in this instance heads and pinnacles, the craftsmen contrived to express the vertical qualities of the Neville Screen.

Although Durham's role as a cathedral has been constant over the centuries, moments in its history have marked fundamental shifts in the character of that role. In addition, there were particularly turbulent periods when the cathedral was used for purposes of a wholely different nature from those for which it was constructed.

The cathedral's early history is one of virtually continual growth and ever increasing splendour, its internal space gradually filling with altars and other architectural embellishments, while its surfaces were increasingly adorned with painted decoration. In addition although the Order of St Benedict had originally required its followers to pool resources, its Rule had become somewhat distorted and, on occasions, was abandoned completely. There were individual monks who were both in possession and in control of personal property and wealth, as is proved by the records of their contributions to help maintain the fabric of the cathedral.

The general wealth of the community and their status in the latter part of the fourteenth century is revealed by their request to the Pope that their prior might have the right to display pontifical insignia – the mitre, ring and pastoral staff – their argument being that they could demonstrate a considerable income of some 5,000 marks, and that lesser establishments had already been granted such a privilege. In 1382 their request was granted. However, as the medieval period came to a close, the position of the monastic community gradually began to change as the numbers living the by then comfortable monastic life began to drop, and their influence and power began to wane.

During a visit by Princess Margaret (soon to become the Queen of James IV of Scotland) to Durham, the last miracle connected with the shrine of St Cuthbert is said to have taken place when one of the princess's attendants, Richard Poele, was cured of a rupture. By this time, it would seem that Cuthbert was no longer believed to hold women in contempt, for Margaret was allowed to kiss the holy relic. Indeed, the powers of St Cuthbert and the cult of his worship were dwindling. The former practice of presenting the saint's remains with offerings of considerable value, which had once been so common, was becoming a dying tradition and, by 1514, it stopped entirely.

Such changing fortunes must have been disturbing for those involved in the administration of the cathedral and its numerous offices and cells, but it was only the lightest of breezes, the merest hint of what was to come. It seems that throughout the country public opinion was turning away from the clergy altogether. This may have been caused by resentment of the church's wealth, but there was also a general feeling among the populace that the clergy should be less remote, and more directly involved with the day to day lives of ordinary people. King Henry VIII was no exception on either count. He looked with a greedy eye on the treasures of the church, which would substantially swell the coffers of the crown, and was on far from amenable terms with the Church over its allegiance to the Pope. In the course of acquiring the church's wealth and destroying its power structure, Henry forced through changes which had more impact on the fortunes of Durham Cathedral than anything else since the imposition of Norman rule upon the Saxon community of St Cuthbert in the eleventh century.

Finely crafted from Caen stone in 1380, the Neville Screen in the choir is an imposing sight. However, though largely perpendicular – its vertical lines exaggerated and tipped with pinnacles or towers – the tracery normally associated with the style is missing. The spikey vertical carving is grouped into five major and four lesser canopies which make both a physical and a visual division between the choir and St Cuthbert's shrine, which is positioned directly behind it. The name Neville refers to its major benefactor, John, Lord Neville.

The Dissolution of the monasteries

In 1536, Henry VIII resolved to suppress religious houses which had an annual income of less than £200 – such houses formed the support network for the parent establishments. Seizure of their wares brought the crown some revenue, but the real significance of the action lay in its curbing effect on the workings of the church. During the suppression, Durham's outlying cells were confiscated and the monks associated with them were incorporated into the parent establishment at the cathedral. Without the network of small establishments, the parent house at Durham was vulnerable and like many others throughout the country, it was soon under attack.

The visit made by the King's men – Dr Leigh, Dr Henley and Dr Blitheman – is recorded in the *Rites of Durham.* Although an undoubtedly highly biased account written by one who was far from being a supporter of the King's actions, it is an important record as it throws light on the way the King's men went about their business. Their approach certainly lacked all sense of reverence, for it seems that their aim was simply to confiscate as much of value as could be discovered. On their orders, coffins thought to contain valuables were prised open, including that of St Cuthbert. The workman employed to open Cuthbert's tomb found the work hard going and had to use a sledgehammer to break into it; in doing so he accidentally damaged the still incorrupt body of the saint. The chronicler records that the workman called to the commissioners that he had broken one of the

ABOVE LEFT Along the north side of the Neville Screen is a short row of seats carved in the same spikey perpendicular style as the front section.

BELOW LEFT Damaged and somewhat crudely repaired, this carved angel is nevertheless a delightful surviving detail on the Neville Screen. Over the centuries, the screen suffered the loss of most of its other decorative figures, including the 107 alabaster images which once occupied its niches.

RIGHT This view from the south nave aisle looking north-east clearly shows in the foreground the chevron pattern of the cylindrical piers incised across the jointing of the stonework. The point of the chevron occurs vertically every other block and is centred in a full block each time, demonstrating the total integration of design and construction. In the middle distance is a pier bearing a reticulated pattern and beyond it one with spiral patterning. The tomb belongs to John 5th Baron Neville (after whom the Neville Screen is named) who died in 1388, and his wife Matilda. Their large financial contribution to the cathedral coffers bought the Nevilles the privilege of being the first lay people to be buried there.

saint's legs and he was subsequently ordered to toss the bones down from the shrine to the floor of the church – presumably because they found it impossible to believe that there could still be a body for the workman to break. The man refused, saying that he could not do so because 'ye siynewes & ye skine heild it'. On investigation, Dr Henley and Dr Leigh found the body to indeed still be incorrupt and furthermore they discovered that the saint's clothing was 'freshe saife & not consumed'. Intrigued, it seems the commissioners handled the body – unlike the former, more reverential viewers of the relic, who feared so much as touching the remains – and then ordered it to be held until the will of the King was known. Eventually, the monks obtained permission to rebury their saint and did so on the spot where his by then dismantled shrine had once stood.

Among the commissioners' attendants there were jewellers who valued the cathedral's treasures and judged what was worth removing. These included a fine emerald which was worth a huge sum of money. In 1401, over a century earlier, the stone had been valued at a massive £3336 13s 6d. However, once out of the keepership of the cathedral the emerald disappeared. It probably never reached the King's treasury, but was instead siphoned off into the commissioners' own coffers.

The presiding prior at this time was Hugh Whitehead, a former head of Durham College, Oxford, who, on 31 December 1539, handed Durham over to the King's men. Whitehead retained his position, albeit in reduced circumstances, and kept administrative charge of Durham's revenues, which amounted to around £1,500. He was forced to pay off all debts and to let go (with 6 months severance pay) the majority of the servants. Then in 1541, on the orders of Henry VIII, Durham was refounded as the Cathedral Church of Christ and the Blessed Virgin Mary. Its administration was restructured through the creation of a new ruling body, the chapter, consisting of a dozen prebendaries headed by a dean. Prior Whitehead was appointed as the first dean, a position he held until 1548, and as such he was presented with a substantial list of financial obligations because while the estates of Durham were returned to his charge, an annual tariff of £218 payable to the King was layed upon them.

Throughout the dissolution, the residing bishop was Cuthbert Tunstall, like Prior/Dean Whitehead an educated man. Tunstall had studied at both Oxford and Cambridge universities and he tended to

Carved heads, commonly seen in many churches and cathedrals, are not an immediately striking feature of Durham, but a number can be spotted throughout the structure. They are mostly found at a high level, where they were less readily accessible and thereby escaped destruction by soldiers, prisoners and church reformers during the cathedral's sometimes turbulent history. The carved head (*BELOW*) can be found on the north wall of the choir, while the lion image (*RIGHT*) is on the south wall at triforium level.

More wall paintings survive in the Galilee Chapel than anywhere else in the cathedral. Though disfigured and often flaking, fragments of imagery – a king, bishop, perhaps St Oswald and St Cuthbert – can be identified (*LEFT*). They are thought to date from the very late twelfth century. The underside of the arch has retained a leaf frieze and patterning which have remarkably good colour – yellow, green, blue and red predominate. More wall painting, this time a crucifixion scene (*RIGHT*), suvives on an arcade wall. It dates from the late thirteenth or early fourteenth century. Other smaller areas of colour can be seen throughout the arcades, over the zigzag mouldings and around the capitals of the west door suggesting that, in times gone by, the Galilee was a much more brightly coloured space than it is today.

abstain from partisanship. The combined moderating powers of Whitehead and Tunstall may have been responsible for the relative lack of physical destruction at Durham, which, unlike other similar establishments, was not immediately defaced and ransacked. Eventually, in 1548, Whitehead was summoned to appear before the King's Council in London, but the strain of the journey proved too great and he died soon after reaching the capital. In 1551, after a three-year period of vacancy, Whitehead's successor, Robert Horne, was appointed. Horne was a scholar, but his ideas were far removed from the beliefs and systems of the pre-Reformation establishment. His was a radical view, and much of the contents and decorative elements of the cathedral were an anathema which he soon set about destroying. Imagery that he thought idolatrous suffered in particular. His 'reforms' included smashing much of the stained glass, and removing the effigy of St Cuthbert. He also instigated the use of English as the language for services in the cathedral.

In 1554/5, Durham was issued with statutes which included the order that the bishop was to take precedence over the dean and chapter, and that the dean should not be elected by the chapter, but instead would be appointed by the Crown. It was also stated that the dean must lead an irreproachable life, and that the prebendaries must be university-educated. Such directions are a clear indication that the offices were to be under far stricter control than had previously been the case.

The sixteenth and seventeenth centuries

Elizabeth I's enthronement saw the deanship pass to William Whittingham, a former fellow of All Souls College, Oxford, who had also been a student at the university of Orleans. That Whittingham disliked anything connected with monasticism is recorded by the writer of *Rites of Durham*, 'he could not abyde anye auncyent monuments, nor nothing that apperteyned to any godlie Religiousnes or monasticall liffe'. He was responsible for much destruction within the cathedral, again recorded by the chronicler, who says that he, 'did cause to be pulled downe and dyd breake and deface all such stones as had any pictures or challices wrought upo theme'. In purging the cathedral of precious works of art, which he considered idolatrous, he seriously damaged the wealth which was vested in its fabric and possessions and which had belonged to the religious community there. The political and religious revolution which had been instigated by Henry VIII's Reformation was thereby throwing the economic viability of the cathedral into chaos. The resulting confusion and discontent prompted the Rising of the North in 1569, led by the earls of Northumberland and Westmorland. The cathedral was occupied by their forces, who ripped up the English language bibles and briefly restored the former celebration of Mass, but the rebels were quickly quashed by the Queen's forces.

The region was also regularly attacked by bands of raiding Scots who, from 1640–42, occupied Durham. They confiscated money from the cathedral to buy food for the Scottish soldiers, who smashed the font and the cathedral organs. The worst destruction at this time, however, took place in 1650. It was caused by Scottish prisoners whose plight was so terrible that their behaviour was not surprising. Three thousand five hundred prisoners, taken by Cromwell at the battle of Dunbar, were sent first to Morpeth, where they were given only cabbages to eat. They were then moved on to Newcastle, where they stayed the night in St Nicholas' church. From there they were marched to Durham, many dying en route, and were summarily herded into the cathedral. Once incarcerated they were given no fuel and were thus forced to scavenge for anything that would burn in a bid to survive the bitter winter months. Eventually, surviving prisoners were sent to New England, where they were sold as slaves.

From the mid-sixteenth century Durham had been in a poor state. Because of the general political unrest in the area, many people moved away from Durham and by the mid-seventeenth century the deserted prebendaries' houses had deteriorated into ruins. Lead from the guest hall had been stolen and all but one of the canons' houses had been demolished. Nevertheless, some buildings had survived in a reasonable state of repair and needed to be used. The Durham Grand Jury petitioned Cromwell for a college which would service the people of the north of England. The jury also pointed out that the government owed the county of Durham £25,633 13s 10p, and they asked that it be refunded in the form of an endowment for the proposed college. In 1656, the Privy Council granted the petitioners their request, issuing an order that a college should be founded within the cathedral precincts and endowing it with church land, which meant all the former dean and chapter's property including all cathedral buildings and houses.

RIGHT The huge, nineteenth-century, twenty-seven light window in the west end of the nave takes its name from a mid-fourteenth-century window described in *Rites of Durham*. Made by the firm of John Richard Clayton and Alfred Bell, it was inaugurated in 1867.

BELOW The rose window in the Transept of the Nine Altars was completely restructured by James Wyatt. It is 90 feet in circumference and depicts Christ in majesty surrounded by the Twelve Apostles and the crowned elders. Recent restoration work on the window has included the correction of contour scaling. The outer stonework of the tracery has been cut back and replaced with new carved tracery held in place by dowels and modern resin-based masonry adhesives.

However, the scheme was short lived because Oxford and Cambridge universities complained that the new college would jeopardize their monopoly. Then, with the restoration of Charles II, in 1660, all impetus for it died away.

Restoration of the monarchy led to a royalist, John Barwick, being appointed as dean, and he immediately set about re-establishing the cathedral which, after years of destruction and neglect, consisted of little more than the stone structure, without windows and with a leaking roof. Barwick was recalled to London in 1662 to organize the the re-establishment of St Paul's Cathedral and his successor John Sudbury was responsible for seeing through the urgently needed repair work. It is known, from the dean and chapter records for 1663, that a great deal of money was needed to restore the fabric of the cathedral and its associated buildings and to re-establish some of the former church practices: £3616 7s 3d was spent on the repair of houses and churches belonging to the cathedral; £1000 gift was made to the king; £566 13s 4d to old choirmen and the poor; and the administrators estimated that a further £3000 was needed to rebuild the minor canons' houses, construct a new font and pulpit, replace smashed glazing and repair the turrets.

However, over and above this basic repair work, Sudbury managed to recreate some of the former splendour of the cathedral, including the provision of highly carved choir stalls and font cover to the designs of architect, James Clement. The font cover exemplifies the merging of medieval and contemporary fashions for, while its soaring octagonal canopy full of intricate pinnacles is carved in the Gothic style, it is juxtaposed with a base that is dominated by Renaissance-style classical features such as Corinthian capitals and columns. Similarly, the choir stalls were designed to combine medieval and classical details to great effect. Around 1683, a carved oak choir screen was completed and a new organ was commissioned by Sudbury from organ-maker Bernard Schmidt, to rest on top of the screen. Clearly, in Sudbury's time there was great activity and fervour, and those men who held office seem to have had a genuine desire to see Durham restored. In the following one hundred years the cathedral gradually accumulated much wealth and prestige.

As this picture painted in 1835 by Edmund Hastings records, access to the choir was through a screen which carried the organ. The painting now hangs in the monks' dormitory.

ABOVE The screen at the entrance to the choir is the third to occupy this prominent position. Intricately constructed from alabaster and marble, it is the work of George Gilbert Scott and was erected in 1876. Beyond it, the west end can be glimpsed, along with a small portion of the fourteenth-century west window. In the foreground are the richly carved seventeenth-century stalls which are thought to have been designed by James Clement of Durham.

BELOW These interlinking geometric patterns of coloured marble decorate the floor of the choir. They were designed by George Gilbert Scott and carried out as part of his extensive refurbishment of the cathedral's interior, which included scraping the whitewash from the walls to reveal the stonework, insertion of a brass altar rail, removal of a pulpit, erection in the crossing of a new ornate pulpit and installation of a new brass lectern.

The eighteenth and nineteenth centuries

In the eighteenth century, many of the men associated with the cathedral resided in Durham for only the minimum statutory period required to safeguard their positions, and they therefore gave little real care to the building's maintenance. The perceived glories of the cathedral were its relatively superficial furnishings, but its fundamental fabric was allowed to deteriorate. In 1777, John Wooler, the cathedral architect, reported: cracks in the vaulting running along the south side of the nave, from the choir in the east all the way to the west end (though no one had noticed it before and on closer examination it turned out to be an old fault); a bulging cloister wall in need of shoring up; badly eroded stonework throughout; towers and pinnacles in a poor state of repair; the near collapse of the small room above the north door; and water leakage in numerous places. To solve the latter problem he recommended chipping away the external stonework to a depth of several inches, but this drastic measure, carried out under the supervision of Wooler's assistant, George Nicholson (architect of Prebend's Bridge), resulted in the loss of much external decoration. Similarly drastic was the later construction, carried out to Wooler's designs, of small spires and pinnacles on the west towers which contrast unfavourably with the bulk and strength of the Norman construction.

Architect, James Wyatt, was the next to leave his mark on the cathedral, for he advised the demolition of much of the monastic chapter house in order to construct a vestry. Wyatt was also responsible for carrying out more of Wooler's stone-scraping plans. The influence of the London architect was great and, despite strong opposition to his designs, the clerk of works was instructed to carry out his wishes and to demolish the Chapter House – a task which he quickly accomplished by removing the keystone so that the roof at the eastern end collapsed under its own weight. Wyatt also proposed that the floor of the Transept of the Nine Altars be raised to make it level with the rest of the cathedral, though luckily this suggestion, which would have destroyed much of the grandeur of the transept, was not accepted. Nor was his proposal to demolish the Galilee Chapel to make space for a carriage drive up to the great west door, but it was a near thing as the ecclesiastical court had been moved to the north transept in preparation and the roof had been removed. Just in time, in response to a great public outcry, Dean Cornwallis was persuaded to cancel the plan.

In 1840, the seventeenth-century organ screen was taken down to create a long vista from the great west door, which was to be opened, up to the high altar, but it seems that the results were unsatisfactory because the doors were soon closed once more. Around the same period, much of the glazing was altered and a number of the windows were replaced with stained glass. Work was carried out on the central tower under the direction of Sir George Gilbert Scott, including the refacing of its surfaces and the replacement into existing niches of 27 statues. To solve the perceived problem of the nave vista, which was considered too long, Scott devised a marble and alabaster screen between 1870 and 1876 to mark the entrance to the choir. Though good of its kind, it does sit rather incongruously in its Norman setting, its highly decorative style at odds with the simplicity of the great composite piers which flank it. By contrast, this was also the time that the cathedral's internal walls were freed from plaster and whitewash and the fine, natural qualities of the centuries-old stonework was revealed. All in all, the interior of Durham, unlike its exterior, can be said to have escaped the worst excesses of the Victorian era.

As well as making 'improvements' to the building, the ever-curious Victorians were keen to uncover the truth about its heritage, and they resolved to find out whether the tomb of St Cuthbert did indeed contain the incorrupt body of the saint, or whether, as was rumoured, another body had been substituted some time during Queen Mary's reign. The slab of Frosterly marble that had been placed over the tomb in 1542 was removed, revealing a substantial amount of soil. Under the soil a stone slab was found, marked with carvings that identified it as having once covered the grave of a fifteenth-century monk, Richard Haswell. Below this there was a stone-lined pit, at the bottom of which was a large and decaying coffin, containing a second coffin thought to be that first opened by the fearful monks in 1104. This held numerous bones, and when cleared out fragments of a third coffin were found that, pieced together, formed symbols similar to those described by the twelfth-century monks. In all probability, the third coffin was that in which the body of St Cuthbert had been placed for its journey to Durham from Lindisfarne. It contained a skeleton, wrapped in layers of silk, along with an ivory comb, a portable altar and, most important of all, a small cross of gold and *cloisonné* work, set with a garnet, of a design and period which suggest it may have belonged to St Cuthbert, and thus offering some authentification for the tomb.

The organ case, now situated in the west end of the south aisle, was formally used as a choir screen. It was made in 1683 and dismantled in 1876, to be partially reassembled in 1903. This section is Baroque in style with sumptous garlands, scrolls and angel heads.

By faith Moses refused to be called the Son of Pharaoh's
daughter choosing rather to suffer affliction with the
people of GOD than to enjoy the pleasures of sin for a season
To the Glory of GOD and in loving memory of
the HONOURABLE SIR HENRY MANISTY
one of the

Henry Holiday designed this 'Moses' window which is located in the west wall of the south transept. Holiday was a great friend of the Pre-Raphaelite painters William Holman Hunt and Edward Burne-Jones, and their influence in terms of style and composition are clear in this work. The window shows Moses leaving the luxurious court of the Egyptian Pharaoh rather than be called the son of the Pharaoh's daughter, and it is identical to one he made in the same year, 1896, for St Paul's Church, Richmond, Virginia, USA.

The founding of the University

During the early nineteenth century, the population and wealth of the industrialized northern cities expanded rapidly, and the idea of providing a university for the north of England was raised once more. In 1831, a draft outline proposed: that accommodation for forty students and a vice-principal should be built on Palace Green; that lecture space within the cathedral itself should be found; that the Galilee could become the school of divinity; the crypt, a hall; the dormitory, lecture rooms; and that the Transept of the Nine Altars could act as the university chapel. Such a complete overlap of church and college would have been highly unusual; however, the proposal was ignored though the general concept of a university for Durham did make progress. The bishop agreed to make a gift of £1000 together with an annual grant of a further £1000, and he also allowed a house near Durham Castle to be used for university purposes. The chapter agreed to franchise South Shields estate, valued at £80,000, to bring in a £3000 annual income.

While finances were being sorted out, the necessary legislation was taken through the House of Lords and on 4 July 1832 Royal Assent was given. In 1833 the first students took up residence in a large house on Palace Green. On 20 July 1834 a Royal Charter was granted, and thus Durham (along with University College, London) was arguably the first university to be founded in England since the Reformation. The almshouses were pressed into service as lecture rooms and, in 1837, the bishop gave Durham Castle to the university to be used by it as a college. Today the castle forms the focus for the university of Durham and, by virtue of its history and its shared hilltop site, maintains a close relationship with the cathedral.

By the late twentieth century, history seems to have come full circle. The importance of the cathedral's architecture is recognized and its history and heritage is valued by all. It looks now towards a future in which the notion of continuity plays an important role.

5 Continuity

Durham Cathedral was designed by the Normans to serve as a symbol of their power, and in this view of the nave looking west some idea of just how well they achieved their aim can be gained. The huge compound piers dominate the congregation (in this instance a St Bede's school service). The internal structure influences the organization of people inside the cathedral by forcing a particular seating pattern, thus imposing a sense of control.

Continuity, an integral aspect of both its construction and its close-knit community, is a highly significant factor governing the life of Durham Cathedral today. Those who are associated with the building have a strong desire to maintain it for the future, and they unite the whole community in the enormous task of conservation, both of the cathedral's fabric and its functions.

The Dean and Chapter

Responsibility for all aspects of the work of any cathedral rests with its Dean and Chapter. The position of dean has an ancient heritage dating back to medieval times when the prior held jurisdiction. The dean is, in effect, the successor to those early priors, his position and powers having been adapted over the centuries to accommodate changing political complexions. Along with the residentiary canons, who form the Chapter, the Dean directs the life of the cathedral. In the past, the relationship between the bishop of the diocese and the prior of the bishop's cathedral was often strained, each struggling for the greater influence. Today, however, the relationship is harmonious, although there is an echo of former times in the way that the cathedral's statutes make sure it is clear when and for what reason the bishop will normally come to his cathedral. In exceptional circumstances the bishop can be the final arbiter of the cathedral's problems.

In the everyday life of the diocese the bishop is concerned with his parishes and their clergy, whilst the cathedral is entrusted to the Dean and Chapter. With expert help they are responsible for the administration of the library, archives, school and other services associated with the cathedral. They are also in charge of the care of the cathedral fabric, along with that of the buildings which are grouped around it and the College.

Care of such a family of buildings, 'keeping the rain out', is a major task. Norman buildings which survived their first fifty years, given reasonable maintenance, tend to stand for a very long time indeed. Any flaws in the construction were usually revealed in the first few years by the dramatic collapse of a roof or tower. The most common problem was caused by the masonry, which, though an intrinsically strong building material, is weak in tension. Lime-mortar, another material used by the Normans, also had short-comings. It could take several years to harden and develop sufficient strength to support the great

ABOVE Now part of the University of Durham, these buildings along the west side of Palace Green were once in church ownership. From right to left they were: Bishop Neville's exchequer, Bishop Cosin's library, the Dean and Chapter grammar school.

BELOW A groundsman at work in the College, the residential quarter of the cathedral, around which are the homes of many of the cathedral's key figures.

OVERLEAF ABOVE FAR LEFT The tradition of employing highly skilled masons is as old as the cathedral itself. And, just as in the past, apprentice masons are taken on in the cathedral's workshops to learn their trade from the master-masons. Here a mason works on the east end.

OVERLEAF ABOVE LEFT Over the centuries the soft sandstone from which the cathedral is constructed has gradually deteriorated, resulting in contour scaling. Drastic measures to solve this problem were employed between 1780 and 1860, when the whole of the external masonry was restored, redressed or refaced. Much of the east front, the north side and the west end had their original stonework scraped back to expose a new surface. Since then, the stonework has deteriorated further, resulting in the need for complete repointing and some renewal. Two masons are carefully removing a pitted piece of stone which is to be replaced with a new section.

OVERLEAF BELOW FAR LEFT Early construction methods employed iron clamps to secure pieces of masonry, but these are now decaying and causing problems. Rusting with age, they gradually expand and eventually split the stones to which they are secured.

OVERLEAF BELOW LEFT Sandstone is particularly subject to erosion, which may be caused by changing weather conditions or atmospheric pollution.

OVERLEAF RIGHT Maintenance is a constant problem for the administrators of the cathedral and a sizeable permanent staff are retained both to deal with day-to-day problems and to tackle larger restoration projects. Here plumbers are working on the lead of the north transept roof, which has recently been retiled.

weight of, say, a vaulted roof. It was, therefore, desirable to work at a leisurely pace, because the quicker building work progressed the greater became its probability of collapse. The main early problem of this nature at Durham was the high vault of the choir, which was built quite quickly and which showed such severe signs of failure that it had to be rebuilt.

Maintenance of the buildings

Today the cathedral has no significant structural problems. It has stood the test of time well, partly because it was originally very well built, and partly because it was founded on a firm rock substrata which has resulted in a relatively small amount of settlement. Nevertheless continual maintenance is needed to forestall serious deterioration in the future. In addition, because of Durham's architectural importance, maintenance needs to be particularly vigilant and of an especially high calibre.

A long-term maintenance plan, drawn up in 1981 by the cathedral's consultant architect, Ian Curry, is now in progress. The plan noted the need to keep certain areas of the cathedral under observation for possible structural movements: a) the crossing arches supporting the central tower, and all movements associated with the crossing; b) the nave high vault and the associated bowings in the clerestory passage; c) the south transept high vault, and the fissures in its clerestory passage; d) the north-east corner of the north transept at clerestory level; e) the western tower settlements, including their arches to the nave; f) the west wall of the nave between and below the towers and the west window; g) the Galilee arcades and north-west corner; h) the buttresses of the Transept of the Nine Altars and its north window; i) the buttresses of the north and south aisles of the nave.

Observation was, however, only the start, for the report went on to say that a number of specific works needed to be carried out, and it is a sure measure of the dedication to the continuity of the cathedral by all those associated with it, that the architect's plans are projected two centuries into the future. He suggested that inaccessible areas of the building can only be scaffolded, for repointing and masonry renewal, every 75 to 100 years, and recommended that any new roof coverings should have a life of 100 to 200 years. In order to make the best use of limited money and resources, the architect specified the priority of each

ANDY

LEFT The simple white marble baluster-type font, decorated with a series of convex curves or gadroons, dates from 1663. Above it looms the seventeenth-century canopy provided by Bishop John Cosin. It stands about 40 feet high and is some 9 feet in diameter at its base. Its octagonal structure is decorated with fluted composite columns, pendants, an acanthus frieze and scroll ornamentation. On the higher sections Gothic tracery is used to create a soaring effect.

BELOW RIGHT One of the more recent monuments to be added to the cathedral's furnishings, this Miners Memorial in the south aisle was assembled by Donald McIntyre in 1947. It utilizes seventeenth-century wooden cherubs along with fragments of wood-carving from a Spanish overmantle.

ABOVE Details from the Miners Memorial showing figures with a ladder and pincers and a small squat figure with a hammer.

repair: 'urgent' – requiring early attention; 'essential works' – to be carried out as soon as possible; 'necessary works' – as soon as practicable; 'necessary' – in due course; 'future works' – those which are desirable already or will become necessary. The 'urgent' list consisted of a small area of fungus above the south side of the choir vault; however, the list of 'essential works' was considerably longer. The masonry of the east front including the Rose window and the gable above it required attention, and was repaired in the 1980s; installations – lightening conductors, fire fighting equipment, etc – needed to be tested; repairs were necessary to rainwater pipes and parapet gutters; part of the east face of the north-west tower required repair work, as did the north nave triforium roof. The nave roof and north transept roof, both covered with Westmoreland slate, presented very expensive problems as the architect stated that they should be renewed as soon as was practicable – which represented a major financial undertaking.

In addition, for almost 900 years the stonework of the cathedral has gradually deteriorated, worn away by harsh weather and more recently by air pollution. In large areas 'contour scaling' has occurred, and several years of research into the causes have produced three suggestions: 1) that the original masons bruised the stone with blunt tools resulting in a separation of layers of stone; 2) that it is due to successive wetting and drying of the stone, combined with frequent bouts of freezing and thawing, a process which is partly to do with the weather conditions in northern England, and partly to do with stone cutting techniques; 3) that rain contains sulphurous deposits (produced by atmospheric pollution) which over the years has resulted in the build-up of harmful salts on the outer skin of the stone, changing its characteristics and thus rendering it prone to pitting. Whatever the cause, serious damage has certainly been done to the external surface of the cathedral.

In some places damage is due to the original construction techniques. For instance, several of the stone shafts of the window reveals have started to crumble because their securing pegs (which were let into the shaft from behind) have become encrusted with rust, causing them to thicken, expand, and eventually split their shafts. A host of other points and problems – reconstruction of the organ-blower chamber roof, improvements to the music library, treatment and painting of iron and steel work, repairs to the arm-rests of the choir stalls, to mention but a

ABOVE Early medieval decorative iron-work on the south door.

RIGHT Much of the high-level space in the cathedral, created by the need for buttressing, was used for storage; this winch at triforium level in the south-west tower was used to haul up large items.

IN MEMORY OF
THE GALLANT OFFICERS N.C.O AND MEN OF
THE 6 8 & 9 BATTALIONS
INFANTRY
ON THE BUTTE DE WARLENCOURT
TRENCHES ON NOV.5 & 6 1916
Dulce et Decorum est Pro Patria Mori

few – testify to the on-going effort needed to maintain the fabric of the cathedral.

Most renewal and maintenance work is carried out by members of the yard staff – stonemasons, joiners, labourers, electricians, technicians, and apprentices – under the supervision of the clerk of works. The post of clerk of works dates from the days of the medieval monastery, when the *clericus operum* was responsible to the treasurer for the care of the monastic buildings. Today, regular maintenance work includes minor roof repairs and clearage of rainwater gutters, but the yard staff also undertake major conservation projects such as repairing the severely eroded east front. Detailed consideration of the project reveals the enormity of such tasks. Masons have to extract sections of worn stone very carefully one by one, and replace them with a similar type of stone quarried from Staindrop and Barnard Castle. Replacement is a highly skilled process which until recently was an entirely manual job employing just the traditional masonry tools – hammers and chisels. It was, therefore, highly labour-intensive and time-consuming. Power tools are now used for shaping the blocks, which does speed up the process somewhat.

Modern technology has also been introduced into the cathedral buildings in the form of heating, a public address system, and air-conditioning. The latter controls the humidity and temperature of the atmosphere in the treasury in order to preserve the special and often fragile relics on display.

Maintenance of the cathedral extends to its grounds, which are tended by a team of gardeners. The gardeners are also responsible for the care of the wooded area along the banks of the River Wear and for the College lawns, trees and gardens around which stand the homes of many of the cathedral's custodians and employees, including its organist. Music has a strong tradition in the cathedral, and the choir – its ranks formed by men and boys – sing about 400 services every year.

The library of the Dean and Chapter of Durham represents a further example of historic continuity, for it has direct links with the early Benedictine monks. The Rule of the Benedictines stressed the importance of education and learning for its brethren, and right from its foundation the community at Durham had important holdings of books and manuscripts. For instance, the Benedictines benefited from the contents of the Lindisfarne scriptorium which they inherited when they

UDEMUS VIROS GLORIOSOS

PREVIOUS PAGES Faded flags and wreaths of poppies in the south transept chapel are poignant memorials to the Durham Light Infantry.

LEFT AND BELOW The choir stalls date from 1665, but they were reduced in size in 1846 and then restored by Scott during the 1870s. Note the high Gothic canopies which rise on Ionic columns.

formed the community at Durham, and which they continued to hold until the Dissolution. The collection was enriched by successive bishops who donated amongst other items some skilfully decorated bibles. Then, in the late thirteenth century, Durham College (now Trinity College) was founded in Oxford, cementing and building upon the original monastic foundations of the scholastic tradition. Almost 200 medieval books known to have once belonged to the library at Durham, are extant outside the cathedral. Within its present collection there are a number of important manuscripts, ranging from large, highly decorated books to scholarly textbooks, as diverse as the classics, theology, and the law, and including early Northumbrian gospel fragments.

The Cathedral's treasures

The present treasury, which operates as a mini-museum, is a relatively recent addition to the cathedral, though it does have ancient precedent, as its name suggests, being the room where the valuables of the cathedral and monastery were held for safe keeping. The present treasury was opened in 1978, with the aim of presenting the tension between power and humility as experienced in the story of Durham. Objects displayed represent a distilled, and necessarily highly selective, history of the cathedral. On show are a range of items including fragments of cloth, *c.*1066–90; the head of a crozier, mid-eleventh to early-twelfth century; the Conyers Falchion, a mid-thirteenth century tenure sword; the Great Seal of Thomas Hatfield, Bishop of Durham, 1378; finger rings which once belonged to bishops Flambard and Rufus; the building account 1400–2, which relates the cost of the construction of the new monastic dormitory; an edition of the first English Bible to be printed, 1535; an organ book of 1638; and, bringing the collection into modern times, there is a set of crib figures carved in 1975 by Michael Doyle, a former Durham miner.

The most significant historical item in the treasury is undoubtedly the coffin of St Cuthbert. This simple carved oak container, which dates from the late seventh century, is the very one which held the relics of the saint around whom the whole story of Durham Cathedral revolves. Decayed over the centuries and now rather fragmented, it is nevertheless a remarkable survivor. Its surfaces are incised with decorative pictures and symbols which have been identified. They represent the twelve apostles: PETRUS. PA[ULUS], ANDREAS, ?, IOHANNIS,

ABOVE This cross, circa 640-79, was removed from St Cuthbert's personal coffin in 1827. Its gold *cloisonné* work is decorated with beaded wire and dog-tooth rivet heads. The stones are all garnets.

LEFT Peter the Deacon, from the tenth-century Anglo Saxon maniple presented to the shrine of St Cuthbert. It is embroidered with gold thread and coloured silks.

RIGHT Mark Angus was given the brief, 'the interpretation of the divine and human economies', for his colourful window, which is positioned by the north door. The most modern of all Durham's stained glass, 'Our Daily Bread' was dedicated in 1984.

OVERLEAF At night fall the cathedral is washed with light, and on a clear calm night its reflection is mirrored in the river Wear.

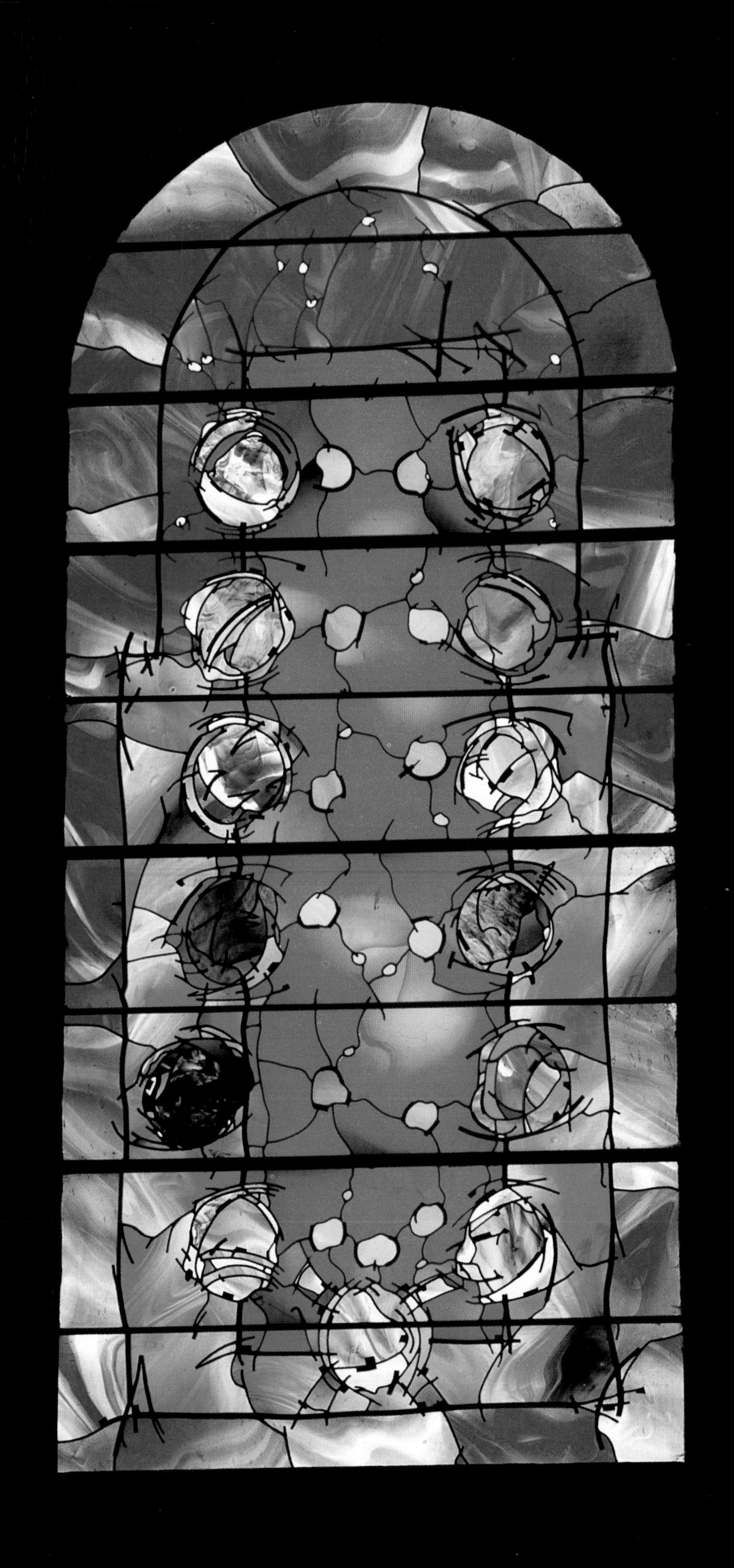

THOMAS, IA[CO]BUS, [PHILIP]PUS, BAR[THOLOMAEUS], MATHEAE, . . . NUS,?; the Virgin and Child: [M]AR and runic inscriptions, *ihs xps*; and the seven arch-angels: [S]CS MICH[AEL], [SCS G]ABRIEL, [SCS]RAP[H]AEL, SCS URIA[EL], SCS?, the fourth and fifth are missing, but another fragment UMIA may mean Rumiel. On the lid the figure of Christ is shown surrounded by the four symbols of the evangelists – lion, angel, ox and eagle.

Care of the treasures housed in the cathedral can often involve intricate and detailed restoration and conservation work. That carried out on the four-hundred year-old Florentine candlesticks which surround the Tomb of Bede in the Galilee Chapel provides a good example of the intensive labour undertaken. They are a set of four, each 49 inches high, carved from wood which was originally covered with gesso and silvered. They have a metal pricket and a metal grease tray. Asked to report on their state, the North of England Museums Service noted that 'the gesso is mostly missing exposing the wood beneath. . . the remaining gesso surfaces are greeny brown colour, the gesso has a dimpled surface pattern in places. . . the candlesticks are generally very dirty . . . one candlestick has been recently damaged, exposing fresh wood and insect damage – the latter maybe alive . . . the candlesticks are standing on the floor on metal mounts but are very susceptible to damage from feet and could perhaps be mounted on plinths of some sort'. The action proposed by the Museums Service was first to photograph the candlesticks, then to check them for insects and clean the wood/gesso surfaces, and finally to consolidate the gesso with a synthetic resin. This would, they estimated, require some 95 hours' labour. However, when they started work they soon discovered that the candlesticks had a coating of varnish/lacquer which was of an unknown type. It caused particular problems because with no solvent available, it had to be mechanically removed – a time-consuming method involving, the Museum Service estimated, an additional 100 or more hours' labour. As an alternative they suggested that they 'remove as much varnish/lacquer from the bare wood as possible and superficial dust and dirt from the remaining areas . . . consolidate the gesso and fill the worm holes . . . the already cleaned areas of gesso will be dulled to match the uncleaned areas by pigmenting the coating/consolidant we apply . . .'. Even for the partial cleaning process outlined, the Museum Service estimated an additional minimum of 30 hours' labour. The

work was of a delicate nature as the laboratory notes of conservator, Hazelle Page, reveal: 'mechanically cleaned areas of bare wood with scalpel, having 'softened' surface coating with white spirit . . . some areas of gesso cleaned initially and flakes of lacquer could be removed . . .'. Meanwhile, new stone bases for the candlesticks were designed by the cathedral's consultant architect and made in the cathedral's workshop.

A World Heritage Site

In 1989, Durham Cathedral, together with the Castle, was singled out by UNESCO, a major United Nations specialist agency, for the accolade of being designated a World Heritage Site. As such it joined some of the great sites and monuments of the world, including the Taj Mahal in India and the pyramids in Egypt. The sites, which span the globe, are carefully selected by an international convention committee whose objective is the protection of world culture and natural heritage; it seeks to promote co-operation between all peoples. In defining a site as having world heritage status, the convention committee must consider a cultural monument to be authentic, and to have exerted great architectural influence, or be associated with beliefs or ideas of universal significance, or to be an outstanding example of a traditional way of life that represents a certain culture. In the case of Durham Cathedral, it was its outstanding Norman architecture which marked it as being worthy of world attention.

In 1972, Archbishop Donald Coggan said of cathedrals such as Durham, 'these great national shrines speak to men of things that are eternal . . . they help us see ourselves in proper perspective. If any one of us cherish any delusions about [our] own importance, let [us] stand for five minutes before the high altar, one frail mortal amidst *all this*, and [we] will soon get [our] sense of proportion right. We do well to preserve these buildings and to beautify them'. Cathedrals in general, and perhaps Durham in particular, are special buildings which unite people and place with a sense of time and heritage. In the case of Durham, the result is a masterpiece of world architecture.

Travellers' Information

Staying in Durham

Tourist Information

Durham Cathedral, The College, Durham DH1 3EH (Tel: 091–386 2489).
Durham City
Market Place, Durham City, County Durham, DH1 3NJ (Tel: 091–384 3720).
Peterlee
20 Upper Chare, Peterlee, County Durham, SR8 5TE (Tel: 091–5864450).
Barnard Castle
43 Galgate, Barnard Castle, County Durham, DL12 8EL (Tel: 0833–690909).
Darlington
The Public Library, Crown Street, Darlington, County Durham, DL1 1ND (Tel: 0325–469858).
Shotley Bridge
10/11 Front Street, Shotley Bridge, County Durham, DH8 OHH (Tel: 0207–591043).

Accommodation
A full range of accommodation is available ranging from very good hotels to simple bed and breakfast establishments. There are camping and caravan sites. For detailed lists, contact the local tourist information offices (see above).

Travel
Information about public transport in County Durham can be obtained from: Transport Information Section, Environment Department, County Hall, Durham DH1 5UQ (Tel: 091–386 4411, Ext. 2337).

Buses and coaches
An extensive coach and bus service networks County Durham, details are available from Durham County Hall (see above).

British Rail
Divisional office – Central Station, Newcastle Upon Tyne NE1 5DL (Tel: 091–2611234).
Passenger enquiries – Darlington 0325–355111; Newcastle and Durham 091–232 6262.

Airport
Two airports service Durham:
Newcastle Airport 091–286 0966.
Teesside Airport 0325–332811.

Places of Interest

Museums

The Bowes Museum, Barnard Castle (Tel: 0833–690606). *A chateau built in the French style, with important collections in period settings.*

The Ankers House Museum, Church Chare, Chester-le-Street (Tel: 091–3883295). *A tiny museum showing the confined life of an Anchorite/Anchoress.*

The North of England Open-Air Museum, Beamish, Nr Chester-le-Street (Tel: 0207–231811). *Aims to portray the 'living' past via reconstructed shops, pub, and houses, tram rides, working farm and steam trains.*

Durham University Museum of Archaeology, Old Fulling Mill, Durham City (Tel: 091–3743623).

Castles

Barnard Castle, Barnard Castle (Tel: 0833–38212). *Extensive ruins of a Norman stronghold on the banks of the River Tees.*

Auckland Castle, Bishop Auckland (Tel: 0388–609599). *Since Norman times the main country residence of the bishops of Durham.*

Bowes Castle, Bowes (no telephone). *This imposing twelfth-century stone keep, which guards the approach to Stainmore Pass, is built on the site of a Roman fort.*

Durham Castle, Durham City (Tel: 091–3743800). *The Norman castle has a well-preserved chapel and Great Hall. It is now part of Durham University.*

Industrial heritage

Tanfield Railway, Marley Hill, Nr Stanley (Tel: 091–2742002). *It was originally opened in 1725, and is believed to be the oldest existing railway in the world. Tanfield now holds an extensive collection of locomotives and carriages.*

Killhope Wheel Lead Mining Centre, Upper Weardale (Tel: 091–3864411, Ext. 2354, or 0388–537505). *A display of mining through the ages presented in a former lead mine.*

Tees Cottage Pumping Station, Darlington (no telephone). *Once Darlington's water works (established in 1849), now converted into a museum.*

Heritage centres

Durham Heritage Centre, St-Mary-le-Bow Church, North Bailey, Durham City (*no telephone*).
Shotley Bridge Heritage Centre, Church Bank, Shotley Bridge, Nr Consett (*no telephone*).

Outdoor Activities

Disused Railway Line Walks

Brandon-Bishop Auckland Walk	9½ miles
Deerness Valley Walk (Durham towards Crook)	7 miles
Auckland Walk (Spennymoor to Bishop Auckland)	3 miles
Lanchester Valley Walk (Durham to Lanchester)	7½ miles
Waskerley Way (Consett towards Stanhope)	6½ miles
Derwent Walk (Swalwell to Blackhill, Consett)	10½ miles

Gardens

Neasham Hill, Neasham (Tel: 0325–721 405).
A varied garden with manicured lawns, conservatory, plunge pool and Italian water garden.

Burn Hall, Nr Durham City (Tel: 091–3780253).
A walled garden on the banks of the River Browney.

Durham University Botanic Garden, Durham City (Tel: 091–3742671). *Woodland containing varieties of exotic trees and an 18-acre garden with display houses of tropical plants and cacti.*

Picnic places

Bowlees Picnic Area, Upper Teesdale (Tel: 0833–22292). *A series of small waterfalls, caves and a beautiful landscape. Visitor's centre with information about plant and animal life in the area.*

Witton Castle, Witton-le-Wear. *The castle grounds have a variety of amusements for children: open air swimming/paddling pools, an adventure playground, mini funfair and a games room.*

Whorlton Lido, Nr Barnard Castle (Tel: 0833–27397). *Popular with families, the lido also runs a miniature railway and has a children's corner.*

Pow Hill Country Park, Derwent Reservoir. *This is a pleasant expanse of water, in moorland setting where there is a bird hide and many woodland paths.*

Cockenwood Picnic Area, Nr Durham City. *A footbridge from the picnic area leads across the River Wear to the ruined remains of Finchale Priory.*

Country parks

Hardwick Hall Country Park, Sedgefield.
Features a lake, the main surviving element of its eighteenth-century landscaping. Good for families.

Waldridge Fell Country Park, Chester-le-Street.
This is Durham's last surviving lowland heath. Public access is allowed to the entire 300 acres of fell and there are waymarked routes.

Derwent Walk Country Park, North West Durham.
A 300-acre country park with picnic areas at Rowlands Gill, Ebchester and Shotley Bridge.

Countryside

Durham Dales
Uncrowded and unspoilt, the dales are part of the North Pennine Area of Outstanding Natural Beauty. It contains many attractive villages including Stanhope, St John's Chapel and Wolsingham.

High Force, 4½ miles west of Middleton. *This majestic cascade is the best known on the River Tees.*

Castle Eden Dene. *A large ravine cut into the limestone rock which has been made into a National Nature Reserve with some 10 miles of footpaths.*

Coast

There are sandy beaches at Seaham and Crimdon.

Further reading

History and culture

A History of the English Church and People, Bede, translated by Sherley-Price, Leo, revised by Latham, R. E., Penguin Books, 1968. Written in 731, Bede's history provides useful background against which to consider early faith and legend.

British Archaeological Association Conference Transactions for 1977. A series of archaeological arguments concerned with the architecture of Durham.

Clifton-Taylor, Alec, *Cathedrals of England*, Thames and Hudson, 1986. A basic introduction to the cathedrals of England.

Simeon of Durham A History of the Kings of England, translated by Stephenson, J., facsimile reprint, Lanerch Enterprises, 1987. Simeon of Durham died around 1129. His chronicle is particularly interesting as it is known that he was personally present at the opening of St Cuthbert's tomb in 1104.

Stranks, C. J., *This Sumptuous Church*, SPCK, 1973. A highly readable account of the people who played a part in the life of the cathedral.

Rites of Durham (Surtees Society, publication no. 107), Durham, repr. 1964. An important and extremely valuable description of the rites and customs of Durham written in 1593.

Maintenance

Curry, Ian, *The Cathedral Church of Christ and Blessed Mary the Virgin*, 12.1.81. An inspection survey and report on the condition of the fabric of the cathedral church and recommendations for its care and maintenance.

Guide book

Pevsner, Nikolaus, *County Durham*, revised by Elizabeth Williamson, Penguin, 1985.

Index